THE AMERICAN HOUSES
OF
ROBERT A.M. STERN

THE AMERICAN HOUSES
OF
ROBERT A.M. STERN

INTRODUCTION BY CLIVE ASLET

RIZZOLI
NEW YORK

Title page: Pencil sketch of Villa in New Jersey by Andrew Zega.

First published in the United States of America in 1991 by RIZZOLI
INTERNATIONAL PUBLICATIONS, INC., 300 Park Avenue
South, New York, NY 10010.

Library of Congress Cataloging-in-Publication Data
Stern, Robert A.M.
The American houses of Robert A.M. Stern / introduction by Clive
Aslet.
p.   cm.
Includes bibliographical references.
ISBN 0-8478-1433-5
1. Stern, Robert A.M.—Themes, motives.   2. Architecture, Do-
mestic—United States—Themes, motives.   3. Architecture, Mod-
ern—20th century—United States—Themes, motives. I. Title.
NA737.S64A4   1991   91-52886
728'.37'092—dc20   CIP

Designed by Abigail Sturges
Edited by Kate Norment

Printed and bound in Hong Kong by Everbest Printing Co., Ltd.

CONTENTS

PREFACE AND ACKNOWLEDGMENTS

An artist has the obligation to mirror not only what he sees around him but also what he imagines, whether from the past or from his inner psyche. Surely, just as sculpture must reflect more than the processes of the foundry, and easel painting more than the chemistry of oil paint, so too architecture must have a greater meaning than that of utilitarian functionalism and technological experimentation. Architecture is not a branch of science; it is not an industrial process; nor is it some kind of cultural radar obliged to search out timely trends and save the world from destruction by perceived evils.

Architecture is an art, one of the primary obligations of which is to create a sense of place, to make buildings that help locate us in a physical and cultural context that is thereby respected and enhanced. It is this architect's pleasure to work within that tradition in a scholarly manner—to be succored by the forms of the past and the values of the culture he serves. But to be succored is not to be smothered. Working in a tradition does not doom design to a simpleminded revivalism or incantational copy-ism. To work in a tradition is to speak a language evolved over time, one that, like all languages, is inextricably bound up with and inevitably representative of cultural values. Such a job is not confining; rather it is the opposite. It is liberating to speak a language well, to be able to say familiar things in a fresh way, and to be able to say new things in an intelligible way.

The American single-family house is a dream house, autobiographical and obsessive; the American household, given even modest means, creates a "home" that is much more than mere shelter, that is an intense expression of personal taste, which, as often as not, the householder sees as an affirmation of national destiny. Americans are lucky. They have complex cultural legacies, being both European or Asian or African *and* American. Mostly, it is the European culture that has had the strongest influence on the forms of American architecture, but since the time of Jefferson we have been our own masters in how we build these forms. Jefferson's pragmatism is evident in his use of the materials at hand and in his efficient use of simple building techniques to achieve noble effects; as seen in his ardent concern for domestic comfort and ease, his pragmatism also helps define a fundamental difference between the American house and the English house, which it sometimes resembles. Jefferson's eclecticism and that of American architects after him, I would suggest, were inspired by a sense of freedom—a sense of being at last at liberty to roam the landscape of an uncharted continent while still exploring known historical cultures in an effort to reflect and indeed capitalize on our cultural and geographical diversity.

I am a modern architect but not a narrow, hidebound, theory-obsessed iconoclast. The modernists of the 1920s and since have sought to make the overthrow of traditional form a requisite of a reinvigorated present. My wish is rather to reweave the fibers of theory and form that the modernists continue to break in their search for the new.

Now, after a twenty-year search, I believe that the purposeful reexamination of the modern tradition as a whole, and not just the stylistic *isms* of modernism, can trigger a new-old architecture that at once avoids the pitfalls of a too simple, revivalist archaeology and a too simple, exhibitionistic pursuit of originality. I try to make my houses eddies of calm in a surging sea of continuous self-doubt; but any success they may enjoy is in part a direct reflection of my confidence in the capacity of civilized people to define the present without refuting the past.

The architect is an artist or he is nothing; but he is not an artist like a painter or a poet. To create a house is to mix pragmatism and poetry, but surely not in equal measure or according to some fixed formula. Twenty years of practice have also taught me that while the painter may work in private before his easel, the architect does not work alone or with his own money. He needs the collaboration of others working closely with him on the development of the designs and on the technical drawings needed to build those designs. He depends on the building contractors and the craftsmen, those charged to realize his efforts in brick and mortar. He also depends on the inspiration, knowledge, and especially the dreams of his clients to stoke the energy of his own creativity.

I thank my publisher, Gianfranco Monacelli, who has for so long shown so much confidence in my work, and my editor, David Morton, for helping to structure this book. I would also like to express my gratitude to Clive Aslet for crossing the Atlantic to visit so many of the houses illustrated on the following pages and for writing about them. Abigail Sturges designed and Kate Norment edited this book wonderfully well. Elizabeth Kraft administered the project through every phase. Randy Correll provided all involved with an overview of the role of domestic architecture in the work of our studio as a whole.

Without the magic eye behind a camera the houses would not come to life on these pages: it has been my privilege to work with many gifted photographers, most notably Peter Aaron, Steven Brooke, Timothy Hursley, and Edmund Stoecklein. And it has been my privilege to have the help of so many skilled architects and designers who worked so hard in the studio and at the building sites to help realize my dreams and those of my clients. Too numerous to mention here, their names are listed in the annotated project list, prepared with the assistance of Adrianne Hachemeister. I would also like to thank Andrew Zega, whose watercolors freeze in time an idealized image of each house, helping to form a yardstick for me and my colleagues as we move on to new projects.

ROBERT A.M. STERN
NEW YORK, 1991

INTRODUCTION

CLIVE ASLET

The title of this book contains a paradox. The *American* houses of Robert A.M. Stern? But he has not built any outside America as yet! They are specifically called American for the simple reason that they could not be found anywhere else. They belong to an American tradition that stretches back at least into the last century—some would say into the eighteenth century. Anyone can see that the style of the houses alludes to this tradition. It is perhaps more surprising to go beyond the facades and find that the planning does so as well. This can only be because the houses have been designed for an identifiably American way of life. What are the points of comparison between Stern's houses and those built, for example, at the turn of the century? Houses mirror not only the way their owners live, or would like to live, but also the things they dream about. How are today's dreams different from yesterday's?

Those questions are answered by describing what might be called the essential Stern themes. It can hardly be said that his houses always look like one another. Turning the pages of this book, the reader will see that the houses are rich and varied in style, often wondrously so. But beneath the apparent differences lie shared values that give the key not only to Stern's work but perhaps even to the self-image of those people fortunate enough to employ him.

The first Stern theme is one that he shares with earlier masters of the American country house: sympathy with the site. Sometimes the sites of Stern's houses are spectacular. Sky View has been built into the mountainside like an aerie, twelve hundred feet above Aspen, Colorado. I arrived by night, and the grid of lights made me think that I could have been looking down at Manhattan from the top of the World Trade Center. I was amazed when the next morning revealed a town I might have slipped into my pocket surrounded by snow-capped mountains I had hardly known to be there. Not far away, Spruce Lodge commands the kind of perfect mountain view that nomads roaming parched deserts must dream about. The house in Pottersville, New Jersey, evokes another idyll: rolling hills and great country estates, with the fox hunt riding by. I walked around the veranda of the house at Wilderness Point, Fishers Island, to the east of Long Island. On every side opened out a different panorama, wild and remote, of bullrushes, beach, and sea. One could easily imagine, with only a little flight of fancy, that the next landfall east would be Ireland.

Not all of Stern's houses enjoy quite such astounding views. Not all of them stand on large acreages. Yet the principles governing the style and placement of the house remain constant. First, the house should seem to belong to the site. The best of these houses have a quality of being at ease in their surroundings, of being almost inevitable, which somehow does not detract from their dramatic effect. The house at Wilderness Point illustrates this well. Cresting the dune, the long silhouette of tower and gable, the silver-colored shingles and sparkling white trim, seem to evoke a hundred images of other houses, half-remembered, perhaps, from the paintings of William Merritt Chase. The house seems entirely natural and right in this position. But nobody could deny that it has presence. Second, Stern ensures that the landscape unfolds to best advantage from the house. Many of his houses have towers, acting as belvederes or viewing platforms. Sometimes Stern has the opportunity not only to place the house on the site but to help the client choose the site in the first place. This was the case with the residence at Hardscrabble, outside East Hampton, New York. The house sits on the third ridge back from the sea, high enough to catch breezes, hidden away among oak woods, the water appearing only as a gleaming belt in the far distance. Up here, among the trees, the exterior trim is painted dark green, harmonizing with the woods.

At Hardscrabble it is not difficult to find privacy. But privacy can be a major consideration for houses by the sea, where land values are high and lots tend to be small. Naturally this affects the siting of a house. There is finally the question of how to make the most of a less than enormous piece of land that accommodates an elaborate new mansion. In England an estate of a couple of hundred acres might be regarded as small; in parts of America a lot of two and a half acres is considered pretty big. But it is not always so big in relation to the size of the house. The discrepancy must be overcome by landscaping the grounds so that nothing is wasted. The Villa in New Jersey is an example of a large house on a two-and-a-half-acre lot. But the site has been so skillfully handled that, unless you are bent on taking a long country walk, it seems anything but cramped. Lantern-topped gates open onto a brick drive that sweeps up, through the porte-cochere, to a motor court; a further, gravel drive leads down to garage and conservatory; around the house itself are formal gardens and a pool. A fountain at the top of terraces overflows and seems to feed a runnel of water that bubbles back down to the house. The terraces have been ingeniously laid out in false perspective to give a greater illusion of depth. Soon tall cypresses, appropriate to the Mediterranean style, will block out any sight of neighboring buildings.

DRAMA

False perspective gives a clue to another theme of Stern's houses: drama. Sometimes there is drama in the setting that can be exploited by the plan. I have described the outlook from Sky View, above Aspen; I did not say how the approach to the house is carefully stage-managed so that the view is revealed in a stunning coup de theatre. The drive winds up round the house so that the front door is in fact at the back, at an upper level. Once through the door you find yourself at the top of a broad staircase, and straight ahead of you is a window of curving glass. The window descends all the way from the eaves of the house to the bottom—a drop of some twenty feet. It looks straight out over the valley. If, nine thousand feet above sea level, the altitude has been making you feel drowsy, this carefully staged revelation of the view will pep you up like a tonic.

The residence on Russian Hill, San Francisco, has a similar stair. To some extent this is another upside-down house, because the panoramic views from the upper floors dictate that the living rooms be at the top. Visitors, entering at ground level, make their way up a straight staircase, lit from above. They emerge from confinement. They arrive at a small hall: "Goodness," they exclaim, "what a fabulous view out over the city!" They walk through to the living room. "Brilliant view, even better than before!" By the time they have worked their way past the bar, through the library, and into the tower, they have run out of superlatives. This house is lucky in having an astonishing view. But by helping us to small portions at a time, rather than heaping all of it onto our plates at once, the architect controls our appetite, keeping us interested and asking for more. He is the master chef whose meal is complete only when the pièce de résistance appears. In this case, it is a glimpse of the Golden Gate Bridge.

In other houses that are not quite so spectacularly sited, drama has to be generated by the plan itself. An example of this is the residence in Chestnut Hill, Massachusetts. The elevations are broadly Federal in spirit, with a dash of Greywalls, Gullane, a house of 1900 by the English architect Sir Edwin Lutyens, about the curving entrance front. (The curve was partly dictated by the need to provide a turning circle for fire trucks at the end of the drive.) But you can throw away the reference books when you look at the plan. It is entirely Robert A.M. Stern Architects. Away to either side of the front door sweep the curving wings. Once you are in the vestibule, a gallery stretches in front of you, forming the residence's principal axis. It is thirty-five feet long, and could have been nothing more than a dark passage, a dead weight at the heart of the house. Instead, a glimpse through a great bow window at the end of the living room draws you onward; and so does light that, in the middle of the house, mysteriously washes down from above. You find yourself irresistibly walking toward the center. There is an anteroom. Suddenly, a moment of theater! This anteroom, flooded with light, rises all the way up to the roof. At the top is a skylight derived from the Tower of the Winds. On the second floor the anteroom—the crossing point of the two axes of the house—is overlooked by a balustrade forming part of the master suite; its dressing rooms benefit from the extra light.

Stern is not generally a man to hold himself back. He admits to the occasional temptation of excess, which he usually, but not always, resists. But his understanding of what might be called house psychology tells him that too much drama is self-defeating. "A house is like an opera," he says. "It has to have a balance between recitative and arias." A house that was all drama would not only be acutely uncomfortable to live in, but the visitor, let alone the owner, would tire of making gasps of astonishment. It might surprise people who know only Stern's more flamboyant buildings, such as the new Disney Casting Center in Orlando, Florida, that one of his architectural heroes is Charles Platt. Platt, who designed Italianate villas in the early years of this century, was an architect of immaculate restraint—sometimes, one might venture to say, dullness. Perhaps so, but Stern believes that his buildings work extremely well, and he has not been afraid to take lessons from them. Of course, he can afford to. The last fault one is likely to find in a Stern house is predictability. Drama can always return, in a more muted form, in the detail. A better word might be surprise. That is certainly the effect of opening a powder room door to discover a classically articulated space entirely lined with gold-veined black marble; or, elsewhere, seeing a window placed directly above a fireplace. Naturally color has a part to play in this: the black library walls of the house in Mill Neck are again inspired by Lutyens, who used black for drama in decoration.

INTERIORS

Even Stern's most Platt-like houses are remarkable for their richness of plan. There are many rooms with many functions, but generally the point of division between them is softened by doors that are either open or absent. Where doors exist, they often disappear into pockets. Pocket doors were a feature of both Regency architecture and the Shingle Style. Stern uses them because, as he explains, "Americans never close doors, never—except where privacy is an essential." Even a house as large and formal as the one in Chestnut Hill has no internal doors to the living room, while one side of the dining room opens directly into the gallery. The service passage on the ground floor is separated from the main rooms merely by columns. The columns stand freely, defining a room within a room, as they do in some eighteenth-century country houses in England.

Without doors, one room flows freely into another, and in some cases different rooms overlap. Spatial complexity of this kind was an aspect of the nineteenth-century Shingle Style. Stern made it his own when he led the rediscovery of it as a living style in the 1970s. Like the Shingle Style architects, he has a fondness for windows that look back down into the living room, so that a familiar space is seen from new angles; both of the houses on Martha's Vineyard have internal windows of this kind. The ultimate example of a room of many viewpoints—experienced almost as though the visitor's eye were a movie camera—is the double-height living room at Spruce Lodge. One stair leads directly up to the master suite, completely separate from the other bedrooms, while another twists and turns its way up, almost organically. The treads may be made from shaped treetrunks, but the line of the stair is inspired by, of all things, Wells Cathedral.

The Spruce Lodge stair is, as yet, unique. Another type of stair, showing even clearer Shingle Style influence, has become something of a hallmark of Stern's work; indeed, some critics have gone so far as to dub it the Stern Stair. This is a reinterpretation, on a smaller scale, of the kind of stair used by Henry Hobson Richardson in, for example, the Robert Treat Paine House, outside Boston. The latter spills out into the hall, its bottom three steps coming forward to make two different platforms supporting benches. Then the stair works its way up to the second floor in a dogleg and issues out onto a landing that virtually forms its own room. Such a stair is not merely a place of passage but a living space as well.

The first of a long series of Stern Stairs based on this principle came with the house in Montauk, New York, of 1971–72. This now looks tentative and rather modest. As the architect's confidence grew, so did the elaboration of the idea. Often the stair has a baluster of lattice, as in the East Hampton house and the residence at Hardscrabble. The stairs of the house at Wilderness Point and the Villa in New Jersey show the present state of development. As Stern himself admits, there may be an irony in this emphasis on the stair, given that in American houses it does not lead to a piano nobile, only to the bedroom floor. Nevertheless, stairs remain, inevitably, "one of the great occasions in architecture." Evidence for that? Stern quickly finds a wealth of it in the movies: "Think of the closing scene of *Gone with the Wind,* of the role the stair plays in Orson Welles's *Magnificent Ambersons* or Billy Wilder's *Sunset Boulevard,* and, of course, of Bette Davis in *All About Eve.*"

Stern has borrowed other themes from the Shingle Style as a means of enriching his plans. One is the inglenook; an example exists in the house in Chilmark, Martha's Vineyard. Built-in furniture should also be mentioned: see Sunstone, in Quogue, New York. Another theme is the tower, which not only gives variety to elevations but provides the opportunity for unusual room shapes inside. Often owners become particularly attached to their towers during the course of design. The tower became the pivotal point of the residence at Calf Creek, around which the rest of the house revolved. It provides a romantic playroom for the owners' young daughter. The tower at Sunstone, stretching forward from the rest of the house to make the best of the views and sunshine, is large enough to contain the living room and, above it, the master bedroom. In the house at Wilderness Point the tower symbolizes the owner's former naval career. More prosaically, the one in the house in Pottersville contains the stair. Towers, window bays, and projecting wings are all means by which a house can reach out and put its arms around external space, turning terraces into semisheltered outdoor rooms, neither quite of the garden nor of the house.

Stern has also shown the way in rehabilitating another indoor-outdoor room: the screened porch. The return of the screened porch is one reason why architect-designed American houses seemed to increase in size during the expansive, and expensive, 1980s. Once they were a familiar and much-loved feature of the middle-class home, often placed at the front of the house so that the occupants could watch the activity of the street. But the coming of the motorcar made this a much less attractive place to sit. So the screened porch was transferred to the back, where it usually stood behind the kitchen. But the screened porches built in the 1920s and 1930s were smaller than before, and people found them stuffy. After the Second World War, when Mother was likely to be without help, doing the housework herself, the fact that the screened porch stole light from the kitchen seemed unfortunate. Then came air-conditioning, which changed the whole picture. The porch was glassed in, turned into a greenhouse, and called the Florida Room.

Recently Americans have rediscovered the charms of the screened porch. Stern first added a screened porch to his own house in East Hampton in the late 1960s, then incorporated one into the poolhouse in Greenwich, Connecticut. Now the screened porch is a desideratum of many owners. It has to be located so as not to block light from the main rooms. Stern notes that the light in the screened porch itself often has the poetic quality of American Impressionist paintings.

Light is another theme of Stern's houses; so, by consequence, are windows. Whenever possible, the house is aligned so that the main rooms face south; the master bedroom, Stern believes, should face east. But this is not England, and the object is not simply to get as much light as possible into the rooms. Some modern houses, with their uncritical celebration of glass, do this, but it can hardly be to the comfort of the owners. The intensity of light in America makes filtering essential. In his early houses Stern made play with screen walls and other devices for controlling sunlight: see the residences in Montauk and East Hampton. They helped create patterns of shadow in the manner of Louis Kahn. More recently Stern has used the architecture itself to shield the rooms, but another of Kahn's principles, that light can be bent and molded to heighten its interest, has remained constant throughout his work. Stern's rooms are often—one might say whenever possible—lit from two directions. In the Montauk residence light was funneled down into the center of the house through monitor-like slots. The attic window in the Greenwich poolhouse bounces light off the back wall of the room. By the time of the Chilmark house Stern's technique in handling secondary light sources is so assured that he can bring light down beside the tub in an otherwise windowless bathroom, via what looks, from the outside, like a chimney.

Whatever the shortcomings of the modern movement, nothing will prevent clients from continuing to want walls of glass, however impractical, particularly when their houses are near the sea. It is a real challenge to provide them without destroying the architectural integrity of the house. The Mediterranean style suggests one solution. The house in Deal, New Jersey, has been treated as an Italian loggia, built at the time of the Renaissance and later glazed in. Something of this approach survives in the Villa in New Jersey; but, since the house is large, a complete system of glazing bars has been designed. A pergola protects the main rooms from the sun.

Light not only goes into buildings: it also comes out. Stern believes that the appearance of his houses is as important by night as by day. One might have thought that creating light sculptures out of dark walls and brightly lit windows would have been easier in the case of his earlier modern houses than his later, more formal ones. Stern insists not. Americans, he points out, rarely draw curtains, allowing the windows of even a classical house to blaze brightly through the darkness.

One last theme of the interior must be detail. It is manifest in the photographs in this book. Look at the Villa in New Jersey, for example: every piece of furniture and every rug was designed in the Stern office. Stern has created a complete domestic world for his clients to inhabit. What may not be obvious from the photographs but will strike anyone who visits the house is the quality of the finish. The suave lines of the furniture, some of it inspired by Ruhlmann, demand inlay that is every bit as elegant. They get it. A composition as high style as the vestibule, with its polychrome floor and bronze tripod table, can work only if the craftsmanship reaches the necessary pitch of perfection. It does. Above all, the detail is designed for human life. It may be expensive, but it is practical. It is ingenious; it has wit. Notice just two things from the pool inside the New Jersey villa. The granite immediately surrounding the pool has been left rough, because it gets wet; but the granite between the windows, where greater formality is needed, is polished. Not only do the torchere-like sconces, in bronze, echo the Roman theme of this room: the loops at the bottom provide a useful place to hang towels.

Stern's only essay in the Addison Mizner style, the house in Elberon, New Jersey, could hardly have been brought off so successfully without meticulous detailing. This can be seen in anything from the pattern of colored cobbles in the courtyard to the Spanish-cum-Art Deco lanterns that hang over the hall and the staircase. Details must be considered just as carefully—perhaps more so—in less flamboyant houses, such as Sunstone. The proportions make the rooms particularly agreeable to be in; but without details like the curve behind the fireplace in the hall, they would not have such a satisfying sense of depth. Oak is used to such an extent that it seemed appropriate for the newel on the staircase to take the form of an acorn; in the entrance gates, cutout silhouettes of the sun reflect the name of the house. These touches inspire one with a subconscious confidence that everything in the architecture has been as thoroughly thought out, not only what meets the eye but what cannot be seen. Stern says that his houses "look solid and are solid. They are made of mature wood; they do not creak; they are well insulated against the weather and noise. These things can be the makings of a sound night's sleep, even when Nature roars outside."

REQUIREMENTS OF THE MODERN HOUSE

An indisputable Stern theme is gusto. There are no half-measures with Stern's houses: he enters into designing them wholeheartedly, and he loves it. Early in his career, the clients of the Lang residence, in Connecticut, said that they wished "to live in a house like that of an archbishop in Bavaria." At that date Stern had not been to Bavaria, but he designed an apricot-colored villa that proved to be a milestone on the road back from modernist minimalism toward ornament. He has traveled a long way since then. A client has memories of childhood summers spent in the Adirondacks. Stern does not hesitate to create Spruce Lodge, marrying the shingle tradition of the East with the log construction of the West. While some architects impose their own stylistic fixations on their clients, Stern is more likely to help clients realize their private desires, however imperfectly formed those desires may be at first meeting. I have heard one faintly disapproving critic say: "They want yards of marble: he gives them yards of marble." But whyever not? Really this should be regarded as the highest of compliments. The people who actually commission houses have different priorities from the architectural press.

They want the places in which they live to suit their own personalities and lives. They are the ones who are going to spend the most time in them, after all.

Each Stern house is a one-off; no one would imagine that his oeuvre is typical of American house-building as a whole. Yet the social historian of the future may well find these very special houses to be the perfect starting point for a survey of American home life during the period in which they were built—perhaps, even, for an assessment of the culture of the American establishment.

The kitchen came to particular prominence in the 1980s, when an increasing number of clients—men as well as women—expected to do some of the cooking themselves. This does not mean that they do not also employ help. Consequently, when the wife cooks, the husband cooks, and the cook cooks, three work stations must be provided. Particular thought is given to largely decorative details such as clocks. For equipment, many owners prefer the kind of stoves and freezers that one would normally see in the kitchen of a hotel; their glass fronts, rounded lines, and metallic finishes combine culinary seriousness with chic. These kitchens must have plenty of room and perhaps be provided with chairs, because of the chance that guests will stand around while the host or hostess "fixes dinner." Sometimes clients require a kitchenette as part of the master suite upstairs, reducing the need for help.

Off the main kitchen there is likely to be a breakfast room, where informal meals can be eaten. Next door may be the family room, where informal life is lived. This will be near the back door and, if there is one, the back stair. These days the back door and stair are provided for the convenience of the family, rather than as passageways for servants. The back door probably connects with the garage, which is itself off a motor court. Except when clients employ drivers, this will provide the family's usual route into the house. The family will certainly use the back door when they come back from golf or, in Aspen, from skiing. The back entrance must therefore be treated as part of the main rooms in the house. In most cases the front door is used primarily by guests.

Many houses possess a home office, reflecting the computer and fax revolutions. Owners may not spend all year working from home, but they may want to have that option for the future. Most clients are busy executives who are "on call" on weekends and over holidays. As ever, the architect has the challenge of domesticating banal-looking screens and keyboards, designed for big city offices. The desk in the Calf Creek house is one solution. The ubiquity of the television set offers a similar, but more common, problem. Sometimes it can be corralled into a single room, perhaps euphemistically known as the library; but what happens when it escapes into the rest of the house? The answer is that, like any other domestic artifact one does not wish to see all the time, it must be concealed within cabinetwork. The bench at the foot of the bed, out of which, at the press of a button, the television set rises up like a Wurlitzer, shows how this can be done. (In one case two television sets, each connected to its own headset, come up from the bench, so that husband and wife need not be separated by the cruel desire to watch different channels.)

American houses have always been amply provided with closets and hanging space. To an English eye, the bathrooms have long seemed luxurious. In both these particulars, Stern's houses maintain national honor. Where he perhaps excels even the high standards set by the past may be in the indoor swimming pool. The emphasis on the pool echoes the 1980s preoccupation with exercise; some houses also have an exercise room or gym. The young owners of the house in Chestnut Hill required a three-quarter-size basketball court. One of Stern's relatively early triumphs was the poolhouse constructed below the house in Llewellyn Park. This spectacular room, glancing simultaneously at Brighton Pavilion, Hans Hollein, and Lutyens, enjoyed enormous réclame when it was finished in 1981. (It undoubtedly had the effect of cheering up, if not quite marrying with, a lugubrious Beaux-Arts house in which the Archbishop of Newark had recently died.) Since then Stern has not looked back. His most striking recent pool is the one for the Villa in New Jersey, in what might be called the Alma-Tadema style. The pool for the residence at River Oaks, Texas, now being completed, promises to be equally memorable, for the lady of the house made the poolhouse a central requirement of the commission. It provides a place where she can live outdoors, screened against the mosquitoes. Elsewhere, Stern likes to make his outdoor swimming pools double as reflecting pools for the house. The pool disappearing over the horizon at the residence in Elberon provides a touch of Hollywood (Stern has been quoted as saying that in another life he would like to come back as Fred Astaire).

Particular clients have particular needs. Those who are anxious about possible kidnapping may wish to have a safe room built into the house. Entirely lined with steel, with a steel door, a separate air supply, a separate telephone line, and a stock of food, this room would, if reached in time, provide a haven of security until the police arrived. Less dramatically, other special requirements include sewing centers, gift-wrapping centers, hairdressing rooms, and meditation rooms.

Unusual rooms are as nothing compared to the degree of technology that Stern's houses contain, almost as standard. This embraces central heat, air-conditioning, security systems, stereo piped to all rooms of the house, even, in one case, a complete discotheque sound system. The architect must keep all these services out of sight. Fortunately classicism helps, by providing a panoply of moldings and pilasters in which cables can be concealed. Nevertheless, ingenuity is often required. The dramatically over-expressed barbecue for the Villa in New Jersey doubles as a chimney for the heating and air-conditioning plant in the basement. The services of the house may be sophisticated, but their controls are even more so. The latest development is to have the whole system run by computer, which will take commands from the owner over the telephone. So, driving out from the city, he or she may call up in advance to dim the living room lights or turn up the heat in the garage. There remains only one problem: how to ensure that your help, not to mention your partner, understands how to use the system.

EARLY HOUSES

To pursue the next theme, history, it is necessary to look back beyond the 1980s, when most of these houses were built. The modern movement banned history. It was expected that architecture would endlessly renew itself without reference to the past. When Stern went to the Yale School of Architecture in 1960—the moment when almost every architect in the world wanted to be there—the first exciting signs of this precept being broken were just beginning to appear. The year before Stern arrived, a sensation had been caused by Philip Johnson's slogan, chalked on a blackboard before a lecture: "You cannot not know history." A similar frisson greeted the appearance of British architects, such as James Stirling and Colin St. John Wilson. They dared to look back, though not to the architecture of styles. History to them meant Le Corbusier, Russian Constructivism, or Victorian railway sheds—the history or prehistory of the modern movement. Still, it was history. At the same time a brilliant, handsome young professor, Vincent Scully, was breathing glamour into the academic discipline of art history, and his lectures were thronged. Scully's *The Shingle Style; Architectural Theory and Design from Richardson to the Origins of Wright* had been published in 1955. The summer homes and resort buildings of the Shingle Style were the common inheritance of anyone brought up on the East Coast of the United States. But by the Second World War they had ceased to be considered *architecture*. Scully gave them academic respectability; a vast neglected swath of American heritage opened up for the study of young architects. Stern took a year off to explore art history.

A year or so after leaving architecture school in 1965, Stern had the chance to design his first house. It came from a former college roommate turned lawyer: Samuel Wiseman. The house sits in what, for many years, would be Stern's home territory: the eastern end of Long Island, which was then just being rediscovered, thanks to improvements in the road system, as a place of summer homes. Reference to the older tradition is made in the shingles. Though the budget was tight, Stern, like any young architect, was determined to make an impression. The site seemed to form the gateway to Montauk, and this suggested an arch—characterized by Stern, perhaps extravagantly, as "Michelangelesque"—sweeping over the roof terrace. It shows the influence of his then mentor Robert Venturi, who had incorporated an entrance arch into a house built for his mother in Philadelphia. Writing in the "Forty Under Forty" exhibition catalogue (the exhibition had been organized by Stern), Philip Johnson predicted that the yet unfinished building would be "one of the most dramatic and 'far out' statements of the latest thinking in architecture." There is little detail inside the house. This reflects not only the prevailing aesthetic but the fact that, as Stern admits, he "didn't know how to do any at that stage," detail not being taught as part of a modernist training.

Stern's second house, the residence in Montauk, contains a historical quotation. The semicircular bite taken out of the top of the entrance facade derives from Lutyens's Nashdom, in Buckinghamshire. Only the most astute of architectural historians could now be expected to spot this reference without help, but that is not the point. In the late 1960s almost any direct allusion to the past shocked the profession. Copying the work of contemporaries, as published in the architectural magazines: that was acceptable. But using earlier masterpieces for inspiration: that was beyond the pale. Lutyens particularly appealed to Stern and his generation because of the liberties that he seemed to take with tradition. Architects breaking modernist rules responded to a man who, in his own idiom, appeared equally subversive. Writing of the house in Westchester County, New York, in February 1977, *Progressive Architecture* commented that "Lutyens is by now rather *de rigeur* as a reference system in this firm's work."

The range of reference buried learnedly within these early houses is demonstrated by the poolhouse in Greenwich. Stern elaborated its many sources in an article in *Architectural Record*, July 1975. They included Lutyens's the Salutation, in Kent (for the slit in the hipped roof), the nineteenth-century Philadelphia architect Frank Furness ("misreadings of tension and compression"), Henry Hobson Richardson (contrast between arched opening and large expanses of wall), Philip Johnson (contrasts of external and internal geometry, as in his guest house at New Canaan, 1953), and Sir John Soane (ingenious lighting effects). Thankfully, the building does not seem nearly as mannerist as this exegesis would suggest. The structure was built to provide some architectural fun, in contrast to the stuffiness of the main house to which this pavilion is attached. It succeeded sufficiently well for the clients to wish one feature—the curving S wall of glass—to be incorporated into the later of the two subsequent houses Stern has built for them: Sky View, Aspen. The interior of the poolhouse is paneled with the beaded boarding, much loved by Shingle Style architects, which Stern used in many of his early houses. Again, this articulation of the wall surface shocked modernist orthodoxy.

It is difficult from today's vantage point to imagine the scandal caused by the application of moldings above the windows of the Lang residence. These moldings were directly inspired—implausibly enough—by a visit Stern had just made to Eton College, in Berkshire, where the Tudor hoodmolds struck him as a way of "snapping up" a long facade. They have the practical merit of deflecting water away from the windows; nevertheless, the fact that they were so clearly attached, rather than structural—that they were, in fact, ornament—filled unreformed modernists with horror. Somewhat stiffly, Venturi and Rauch had previously used attached moldings on their North Penn Visiting Nurse Association, but Stern added a note of panache that seemed, at the time, almost Baroque. There was talk of Borromini.

The New York townhouse, of 1973–75, is a step toward classicism. Unmistakable pilasters stand to either side of the facade, the top of which hints at a pediment. This facade is totally new. Behind it, however, parts of an earlier row house were retained, including, on the ground floor, a doctor's consulting room. The need to circumvent this remnant inspired a *promenade architecturale* that still pleases critics who are otherwise uncertain of Stern's later romance with history. Spatial complexity, as we have seen, has remained a theme of Stern's work, though the more leisurely character of a

21

spreading country house makes this New York level of intensity, necessitated by a relatively cramped lot, inappropriate.

The same year saw the arrival of the column. Stern had already applied a column or two to the outside of some houses, but never symmetrically, never inside. In the remodeled carriage house in East Hampton the main room has four palpable columns supporting beams, in a completely classical way. It was the prior existence of one of the beams that suggested their use. The owners, returning from a skiing trip, were taken aback to see them in place: at this date classical detailing still seemed eccentric in the extreme. Nevertheless, they have become so thoroughly reconciled to them that they have kept the house in precisely the condition that Stern left it. At Points of View, Mount Desert Island, Maine, Stern did not even have the excuse of a beam, since the previous dwelling had burned down. Columns are used to define the principal living space in an otherwise free-flowing house. Their somewhat rudimentary form reflects the rustic character of the architecture, expressed in the massive stone lintel over the fireplace. This lintel is a forerunner of the even more heroic version (apparently random but in fact precisely designed) at Spruce Lodge.

MATURITY

Points of View represents Stern's first attempt to make a Shingle Style house. It is remarkable for being straight; as Stern commented in *Architectural Record*, it was the first time that he had built in the Shingle Style without trying to "one-up the Shingle Style." The taste for jokes, for postmodern surprises, sometimes even an excess of cleverness, took a while to die. In the house in East Hampton, begun as late as 1980, Stern seems not quite to have been able to bring himself to design a conventional pediment over the entrance door, while the way in which the garden front's conical roof is sliced off behind—allowing, characteristically, a second source of light to penetrate the interior—perhaps shows an architect trying a little too hard. The first building that revealed Stern as having emerged from postmodernism into a more comfortable relationship with his sources was the house in East Quogue, New York, of 1979–81. It belongs to a long architectural tradition of small but highly architectural pavilions. There are no jokes: almost every detail has its prototype in the Shingle Style of the last century. Yet the form of the building, with its tall roof and overscale dormers, is new. Stern has worked his way inside the tradition; he is not copying it, but using it creatively. The building quickly became something of an icon of taste.

Different buildings show different sources. The low, all-encompassing gables of the houses in Chilmark and Farm Neck, Martha's Vineyard, have their origin in McKim, Mead and White's famous Low House. Lutyens reappears in the house in Mill Neck, Long Island, its triple gable recalling Tigbourne Court. The Chestnut Hill house owes something to the Governor Gore House at nearby Waltham, Massachusetts, attributed (doubtfully) to Bulfinch. Sir John Soane (Pitzhanger Manor) and C. R. Cockerell (the Ashmolean Museum) might dispute the source for the giant Ionic order fronting the house in Hewlett Harbor, Long Island. The interior of the River Oaks residence pays tribute to John Staub, the architect who came to Houston in 1921 as Harry T. Lindeberg's Texas representative. For the house at Hardscrabble, Stern experimented with the decorative cutting of shingles, which was a feature of so many Victorian houses.

There is no need to stress the diversity of these buildings: anyone turning the pages of this book will see it. Stern has run after history and caught it. The rest, as you might say, is history. But Stern is still running; despite the deceptively calm appearance of his houses, he himself never stands still. The man who rejoiced in being one of the *enfants terribles* of postmodernism still continues to surprise, even to shock. The most remarkable aspect of this book is to see how far he has journeyed in the relatively short time between the late 1970s and the present. Where will Stern be in the year 2000, or 2010? This is not only a question of style; the answer will depend also upon how Americans want to live. Perhaps the 1990s will be as much a decade of change as the 1980s. If they are, Stern will change with them.

COUNTRY AND SUBURBAN HOUSES

Residence
Llewellyn Park, New Jersey, 1979–81

Entrance elevation

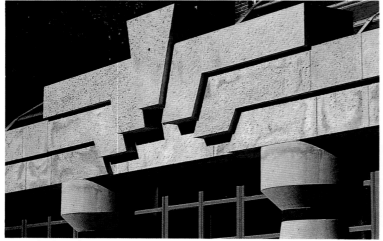

Detail of pool grotto

Garden elevation and pool grotto

SOUTH ELEVATION

SECTION

0 2 4   8   16   32 feet

SITE PLAN

0 20 40   80   160 feet

RESIDENCE

LLEWELLYN PARK, NEW JERSEY

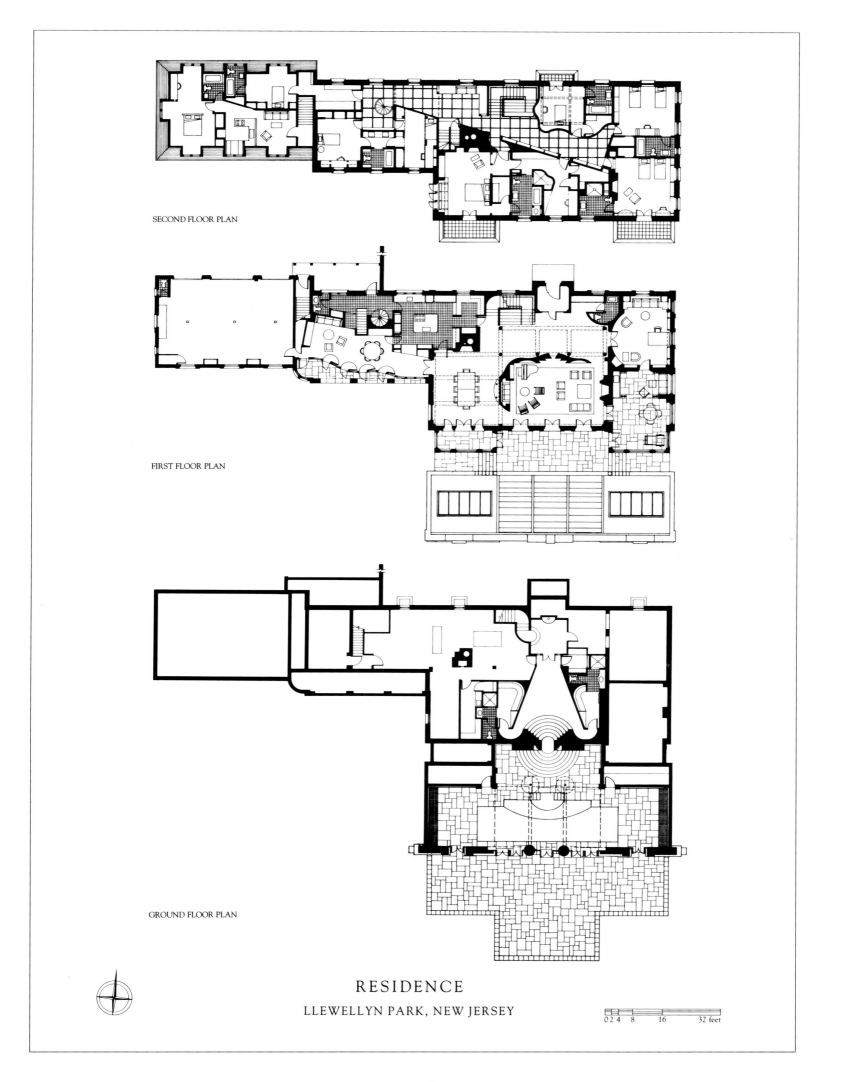

SECOND FLOOR PLAN

FIRST FLOOR PLAN

GROUND FLOOR PLAN

RESIDENCE

LLEWELLYN PARK, NEW JERSEY

0 2 4   8   16   32 feet

Living room

Dining room

Library

Second-floor bedroom hallway

Pool

View from pool to garden

View from pool to house

Entrance elevation

Residence
Mill Neck, New York, 1981–83

Entrance

View of northwest corner

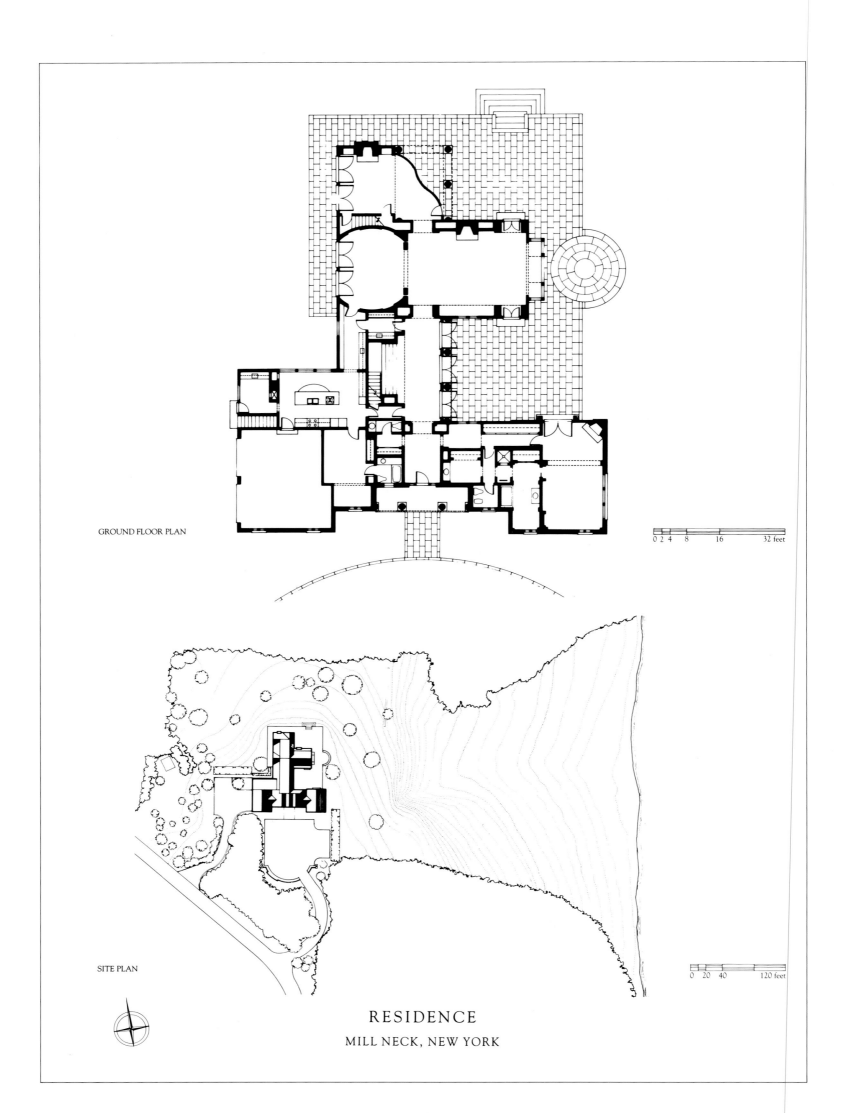

GROUND FLOOR PLAN

0 2 4 8   16   32 feet

SITE PLAN

0   20   40   120 feet

RESIDENCE

MILL NECK, NEW YORK

Stair hall

View through living room window

Living room

Library

View from northeast

Residence at Hardscrabble
East Hampton, New York, 1983–85

West elevation

Pool cabana

Garden elevation

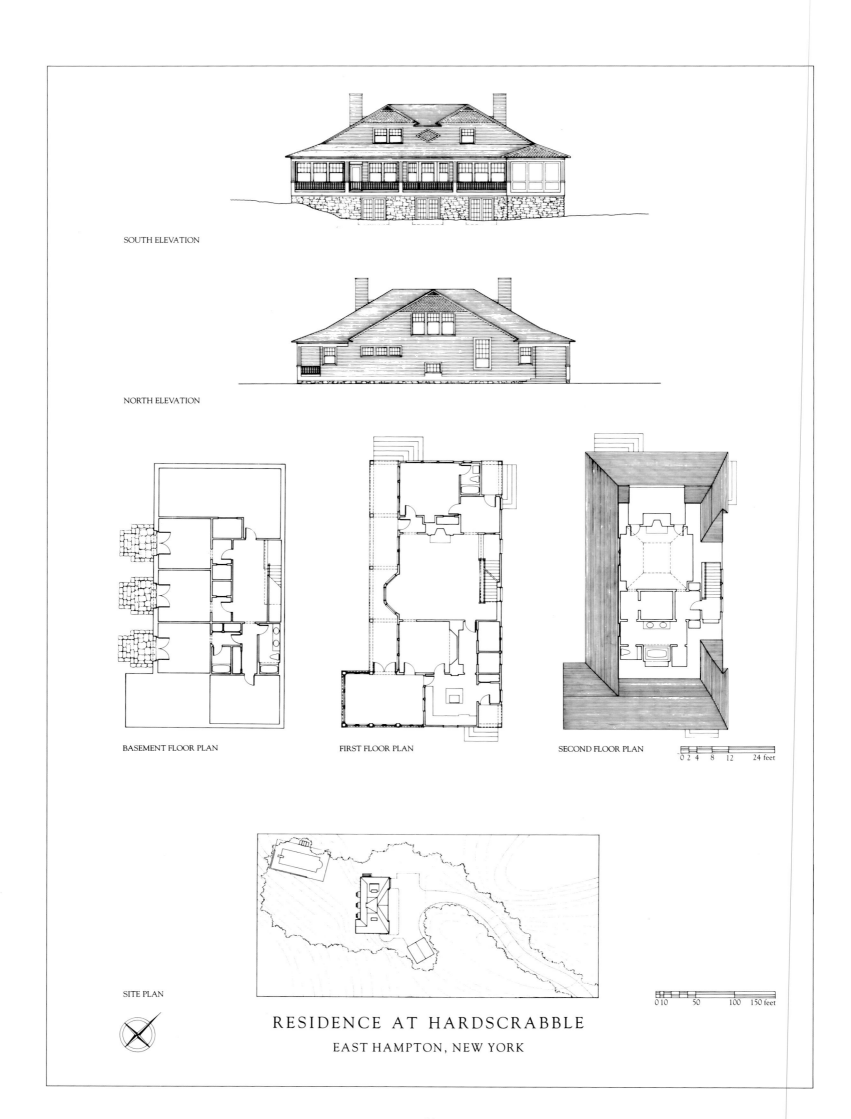

SOUTH ELEVATION

NORTH ELEVATION

BASEMENT FLOOR PLAN

FIRST FLOOR PLAN

SECOND FLOOR PLAN

0 2 4   8   12   24 feet

SITE PLAN

0 10   50   100 150 feet

RESIDENCE AT HARDSCRABBLE

EAST HAMPTON, NEW YORK

Screened porch

Detail of stair

View of stair from foyer

View from pool area

Detail of south elevation

Residence at Pottersville
Bedminster Township, New Jersey, 1985–88

East elevation

Approach to house

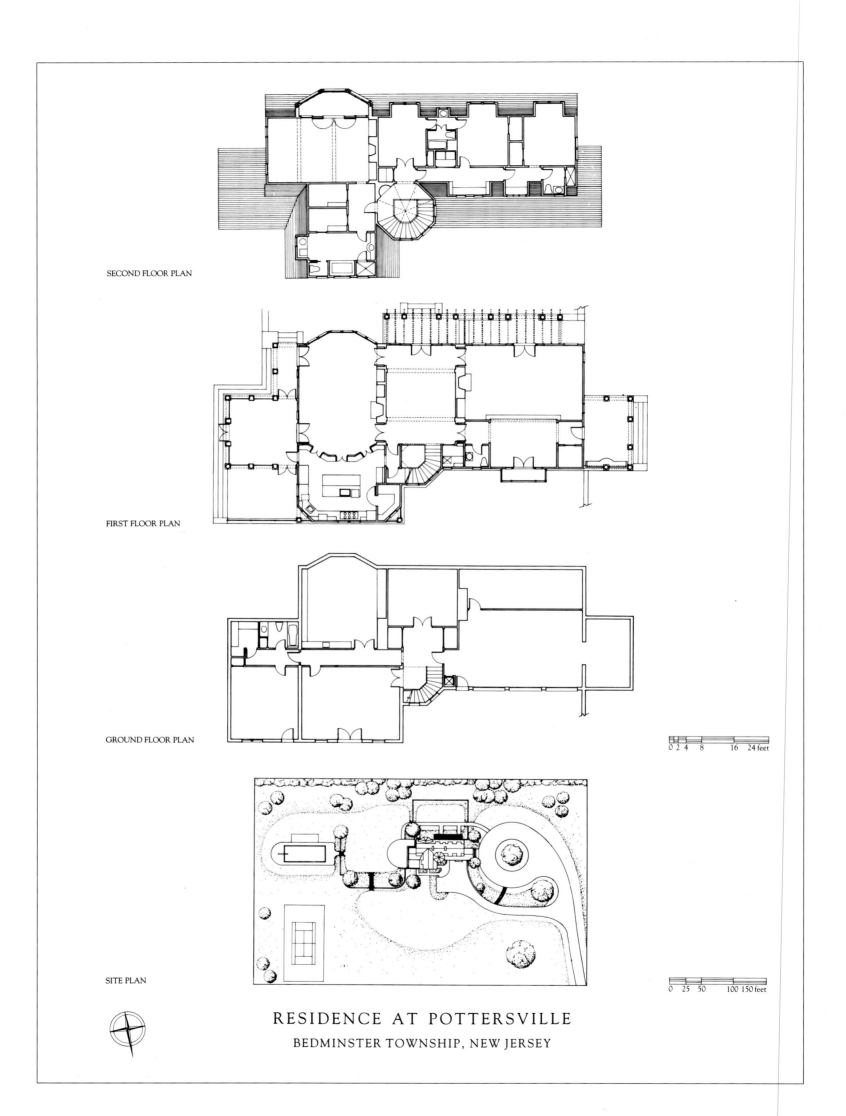

SECOND FLOOR PLAN

FIRST FLOOR PLAN

GROUND FLOOR PLAN

0 2 4   8   16   24 feet

SITE PLAN

0   25   50   100 150 feet

RESIDENCE AT POTTERSVILLE

BEDMINSTER TOWNSHIP, NEW JERSEY

NORTH ELEVATION

SECTION AT STAIR TOWER

WEST ELEVATION

EAST ELEVATION

SOUTH ELEVATION

RESIDENCE AT POTTERSVILLE

BEDMINSTER TOWNSHIP, NEW JERSEY

0 2 4   8   16   24 feet

51

Garden elevation

Detail of pergola

Living room

Master bedroom

Detail of family room

Residence
Chestnut Hill, Massachusetts, 1986–91

Garden elevation

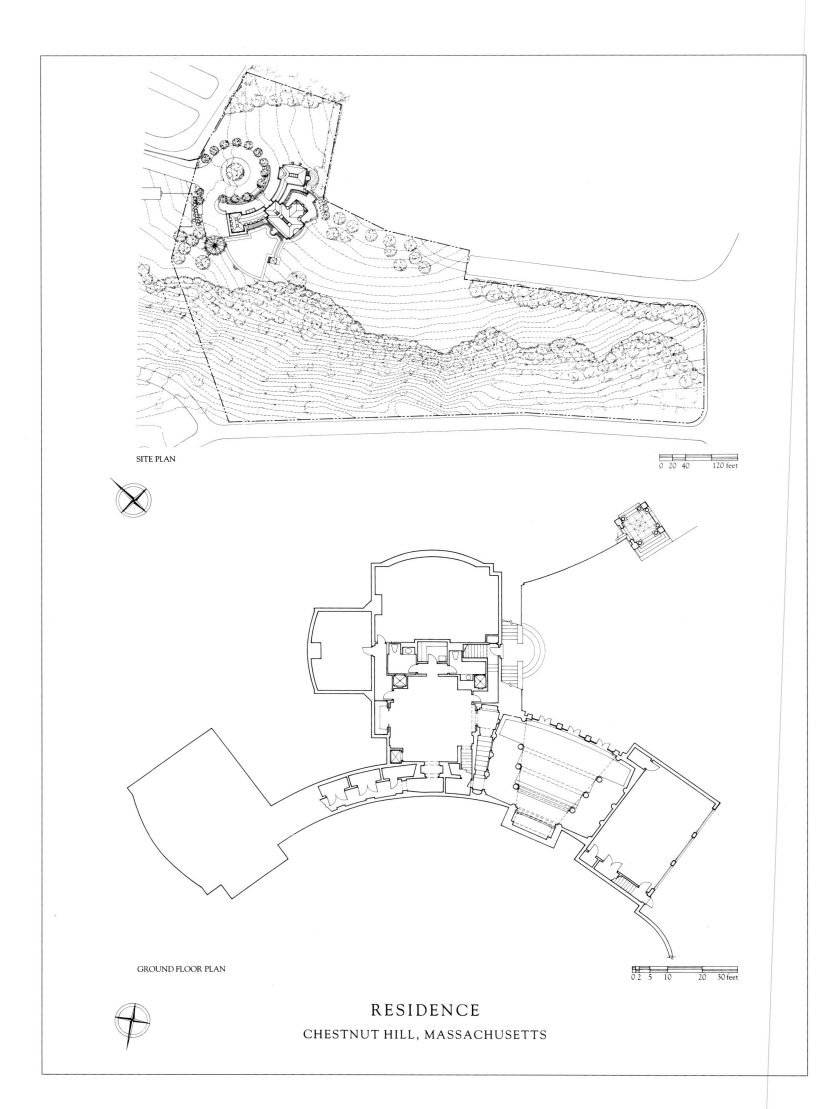

SITE PLAN

0 20 40   120 feet

GROUND FLOOR PLAN

0 2 5   10   20   30 feet

RESIDENCE
CHESTNUT HILL, MASSACHUSETTS

58

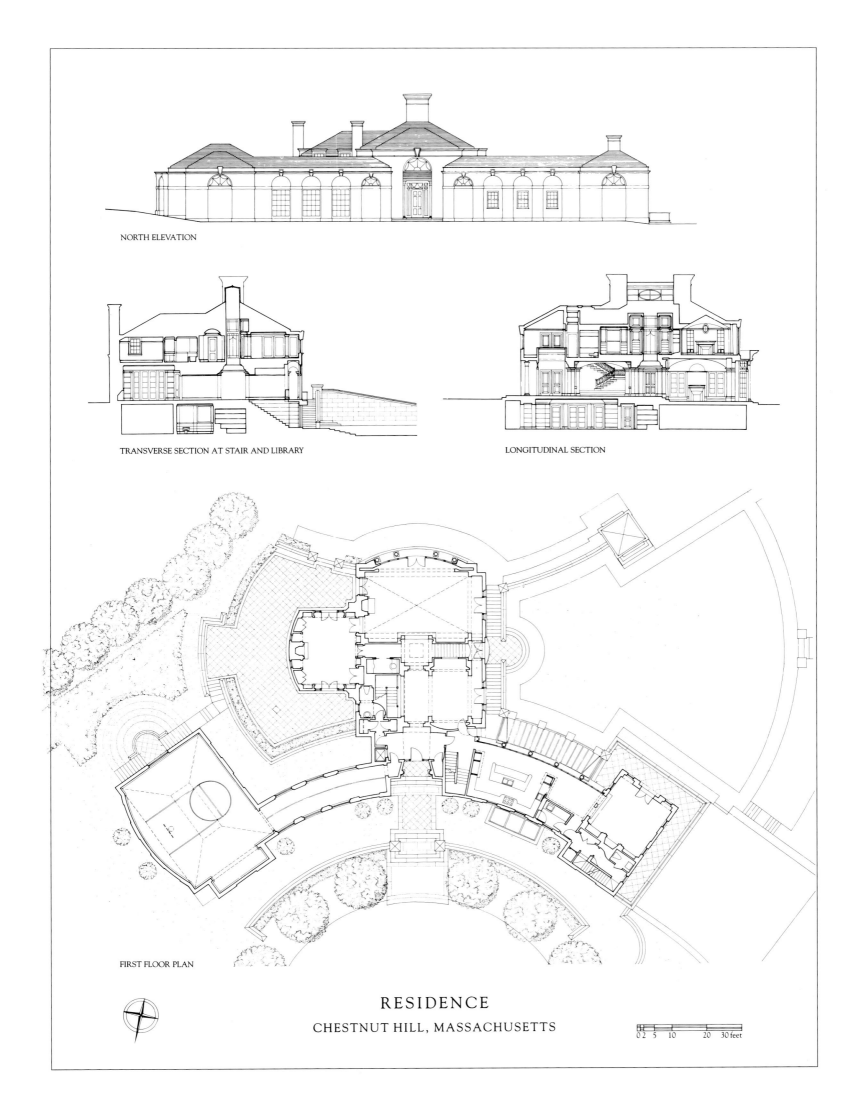

NORTH ELEVATION

TRANSVERSE SECTION AT STAIR AND LIBRARY

LONGITUDINAL SECTION

FIRST FLOOR PLAN

RESIDENCE

CHESTNUT HILL, MASSACHUSETTS

0 2 5   10   20   30 feet

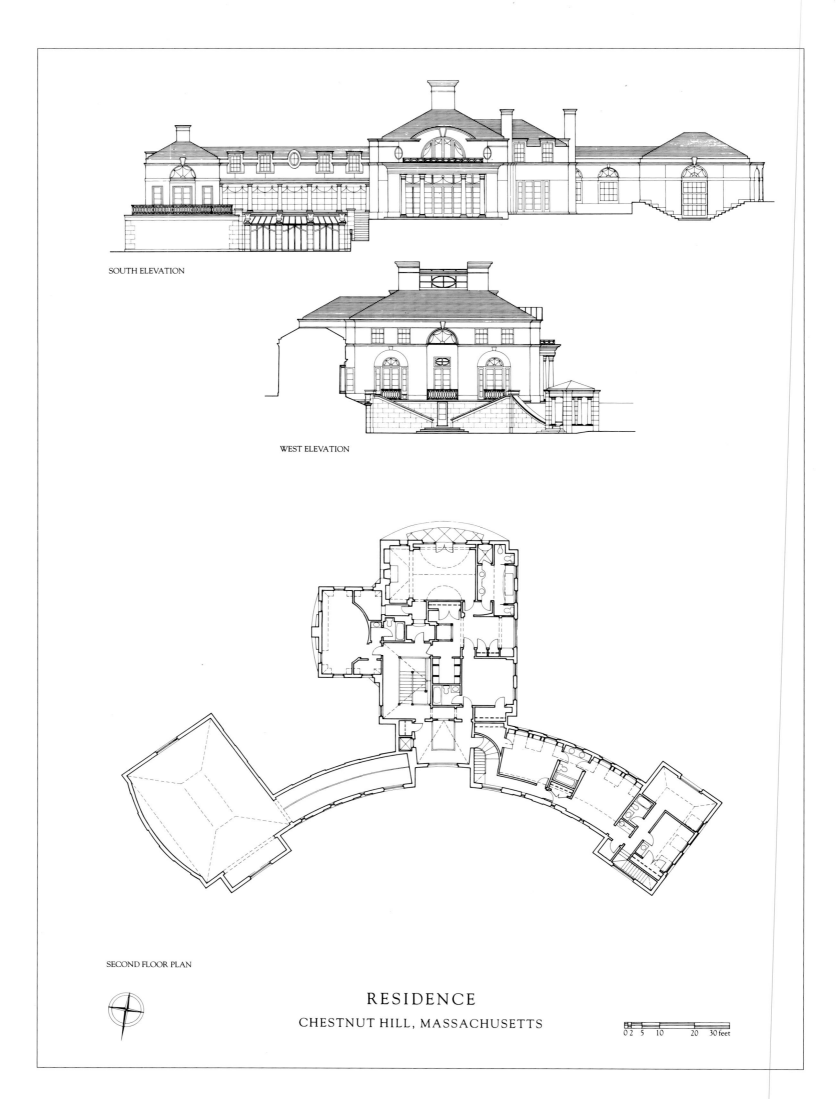

SOUTH ELEVATION

WEST ELEVATION

SECOND FLOOR PLAN

RESIDENCE

CHESTNUT HILL, MASSACHUSETTS

0 2 5 10   20   30 feet

60

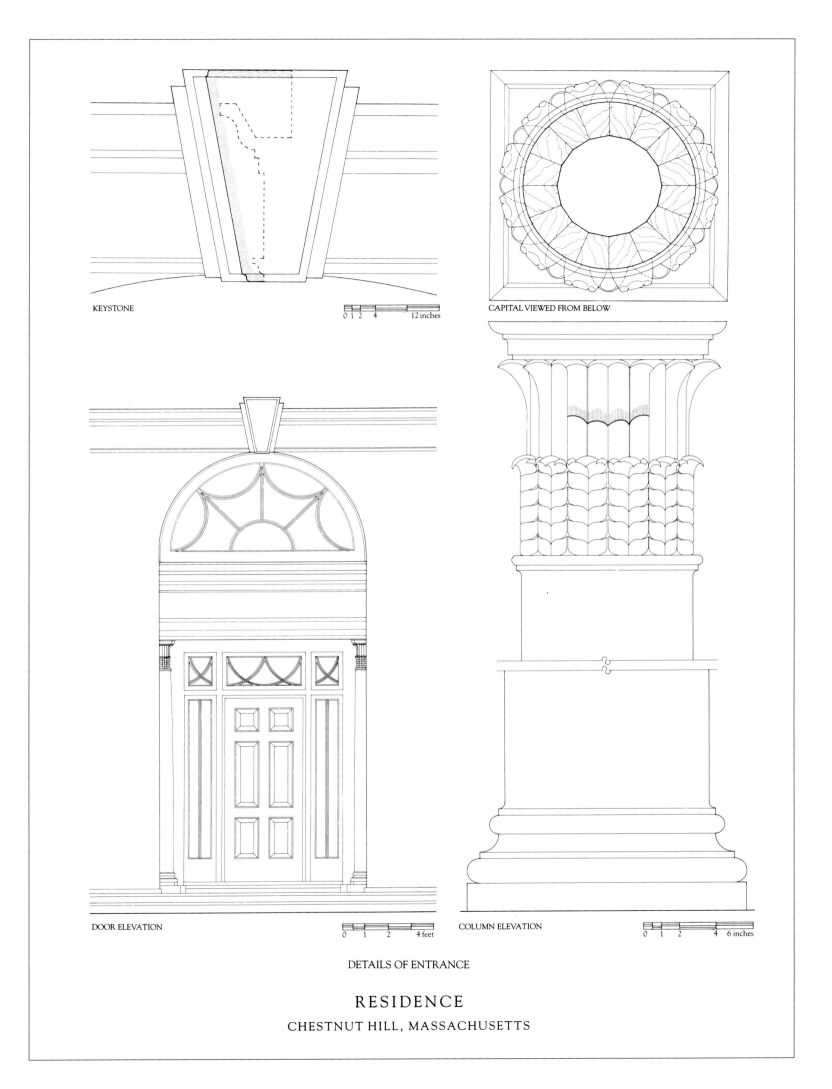

KEYSTONE

0 1 2 4   12 inches

CAPITAL VIEWED FROM BELOW

DOOR ELEVATION

0 1   2   4 feet

COLUMN ELEVATION

0 1   2   4   6 inches

DETAILS OF ENTRANCE

RESIDENCE

CHESTNUT HILL, MASSACHUSETTS

Residence at River Oaks
Houston, Texas, 1988–91

Entrance elevation

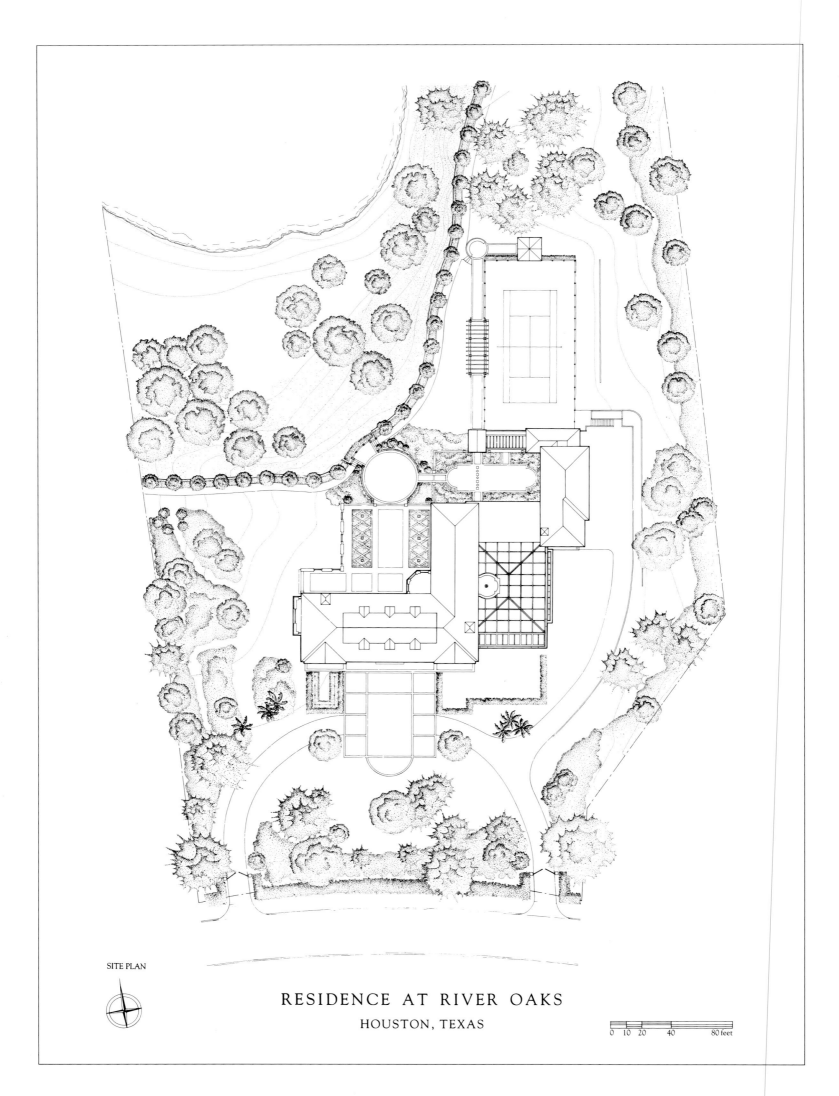

SITE PLAN

RESIDENCE AT RIVER OAKS

HOUSTON, TEXAS

0 10 20   40   80 feet

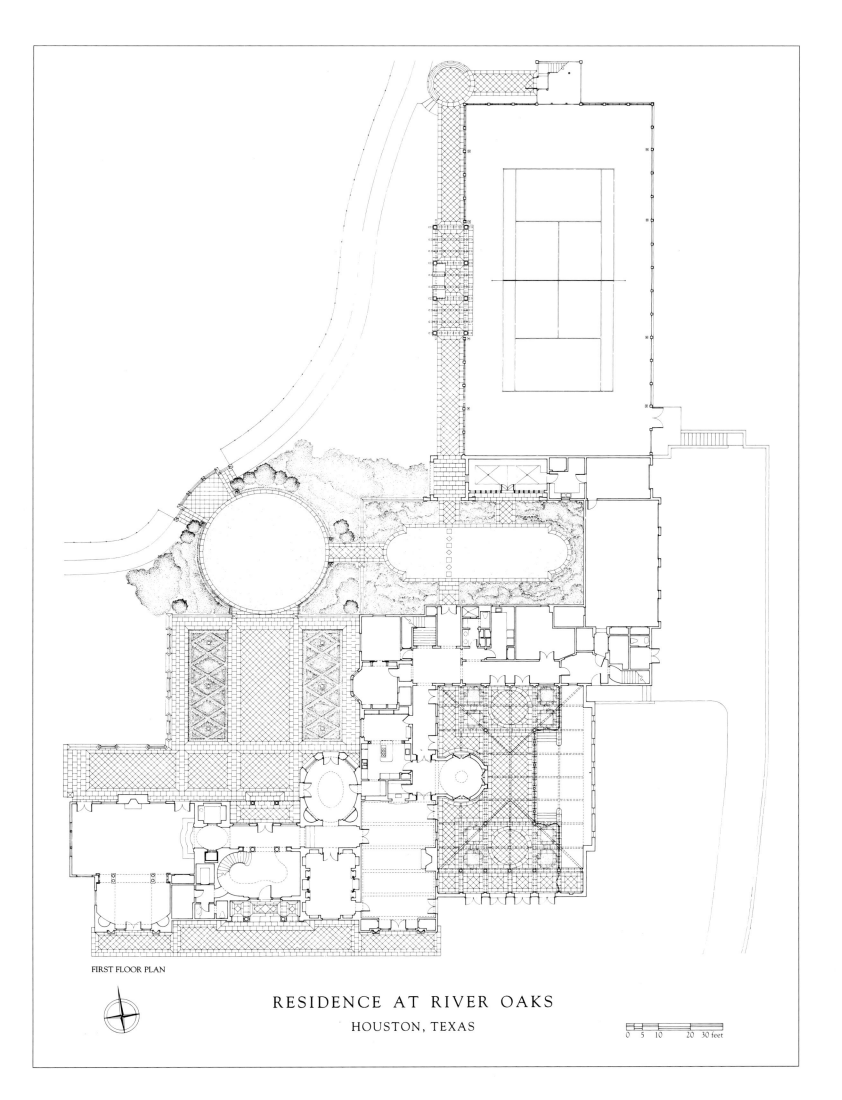

FIRST FLOOR PLAN

RESIDENCE AT RIVER OAKS

HOUSTON, TEXAS

0   5   10   20   30 feet

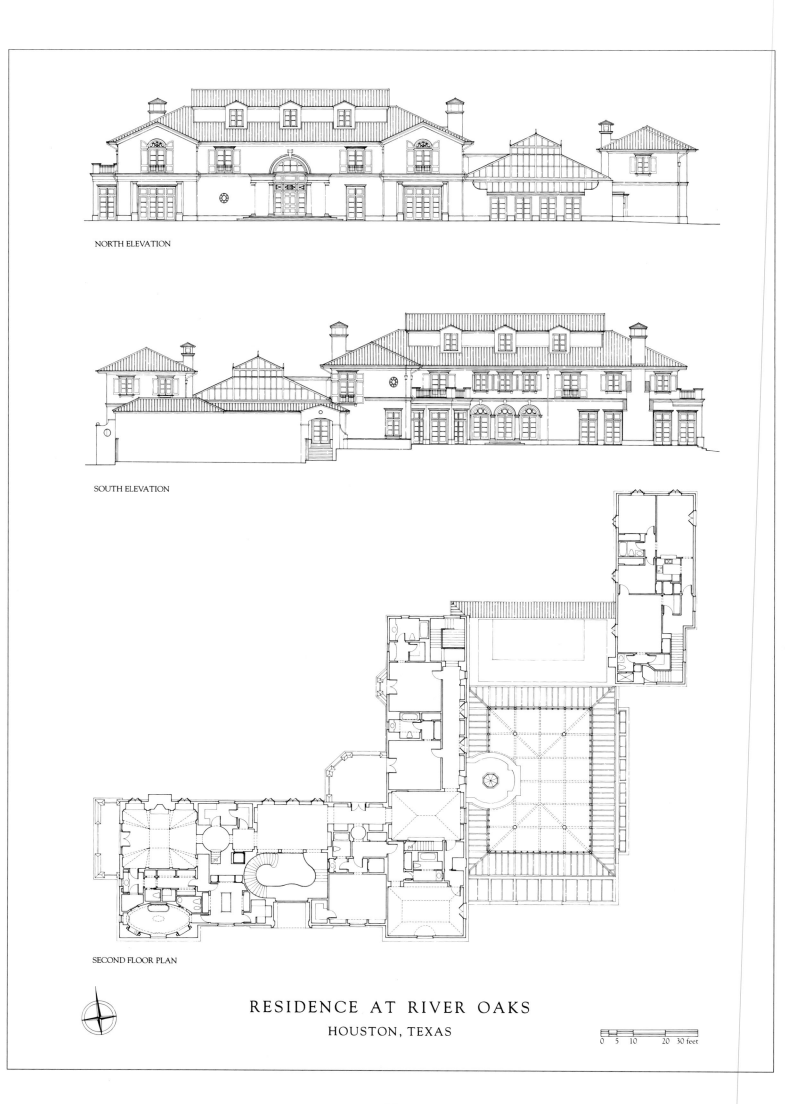

NORTH ELEVATION

SOUTH ELEVATION

SECOND FLOOR PLAN

RESIDENCE AT RIVER OAKS
HOUSTON, TEXAS

0 5 10 20 30 feet

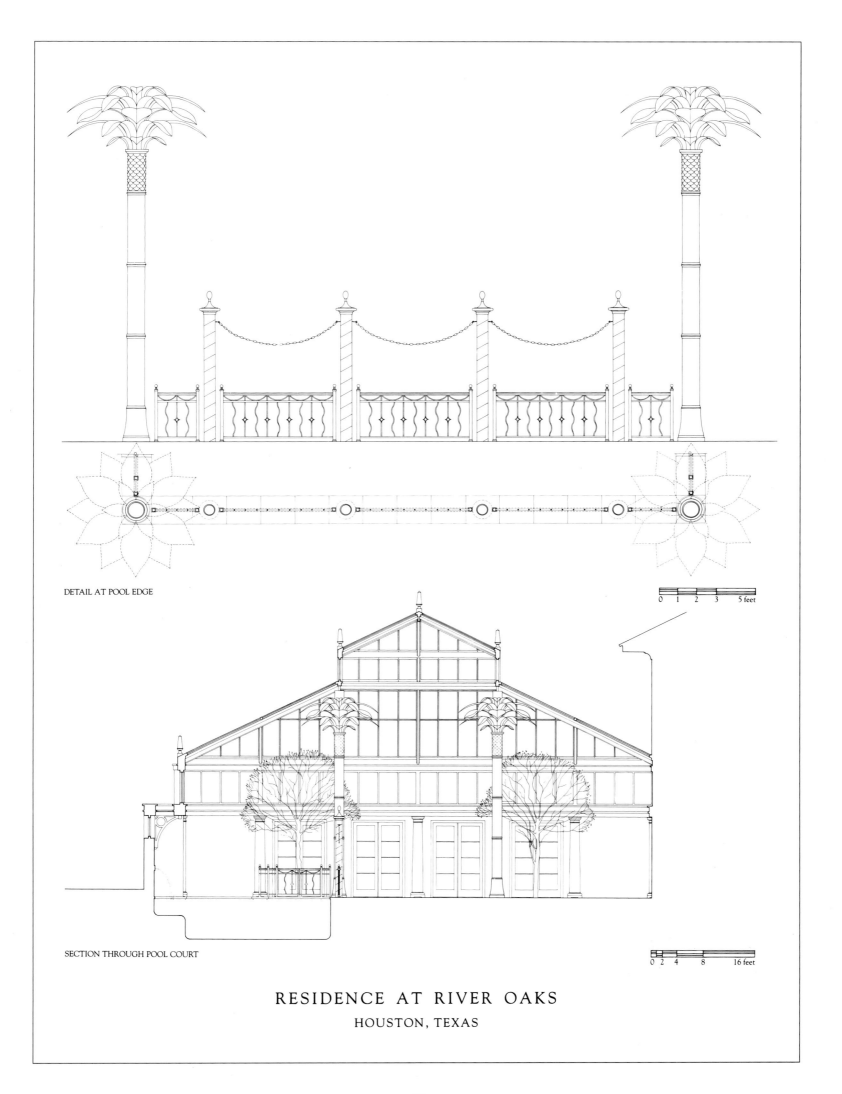

DETAIL AT POOL EDGE

0 1 2 3   5 feet

SECTION THROUGH POOL COURT

0 2 4   8   16 feet

RESIDENCE AT RIVER OAKS

HOUSTON, TEXAS

HOUSES BY THE SEA

Residence
East Quogue, New York, 1979–81

Entrance elevation

View from beach

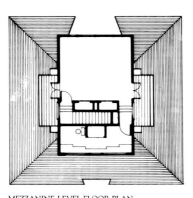

MEZZANINE-LEVEL FLOOR PLAN

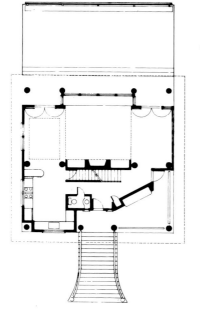

FIRST FLOOR PLAN

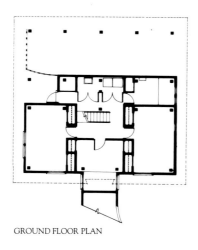

GROUND FLOOR PLAN

SITE PLAN

0 25 50   100 150 feet

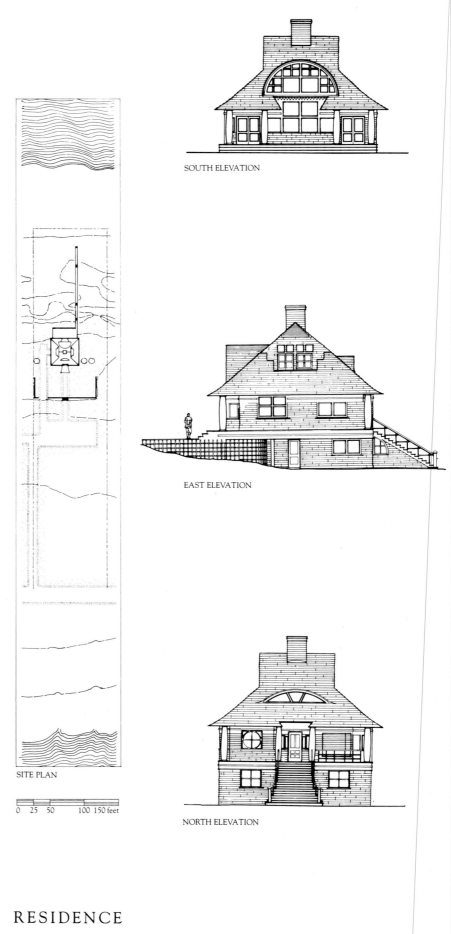

SOUTH ELEVATION

EAST ELEVATION

NORTH ELEVATION

RESIDENCE

EAST QUOGUE, NEW YORK

0 4 8   16   24 feet

Master bedroom

View from southwest

Entrance elevation

Residence at Chilmark
Martha's Vineyard, Massachusetts, 1979–83

Detail at entrance

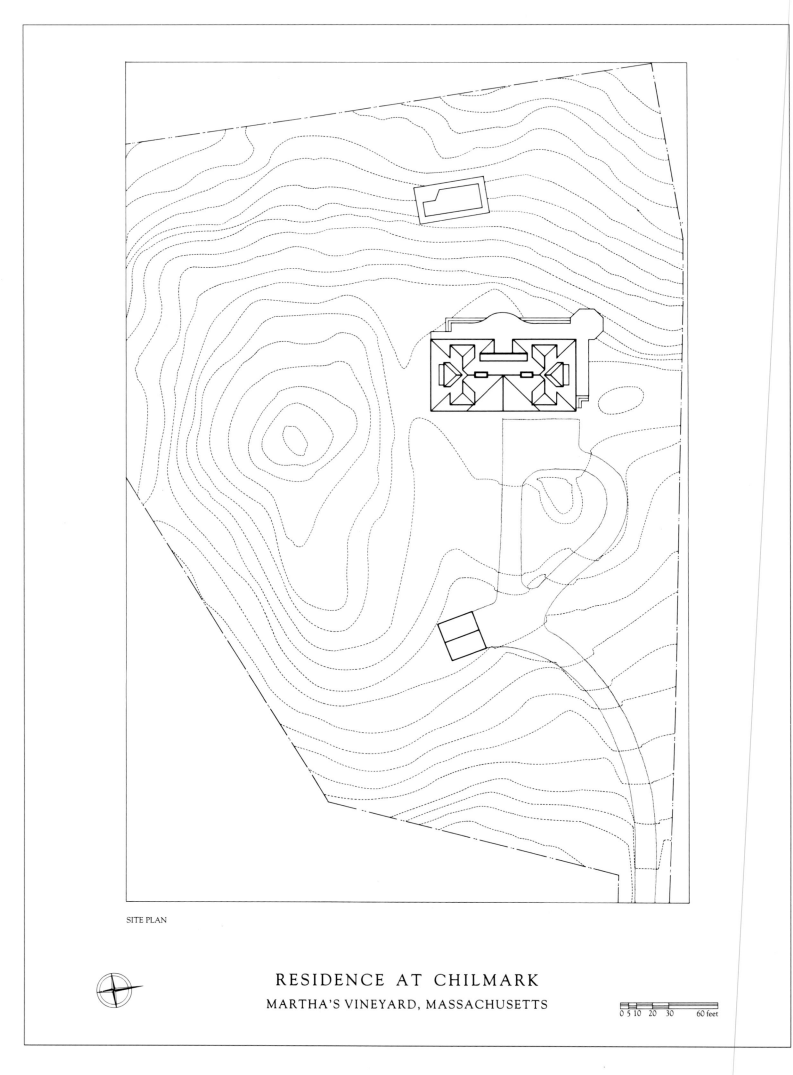

SITE PLAN

RESIDENCE AT CHILMARK
MARTHA'S VINEYARD, MASSACHUSETTS

0 5 10 20 30   60 feet

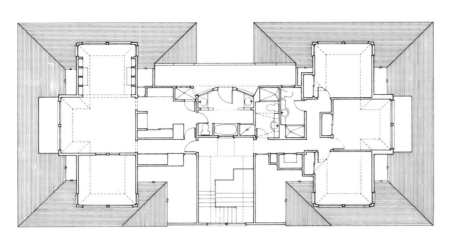

SECOND FLOOR PLAN

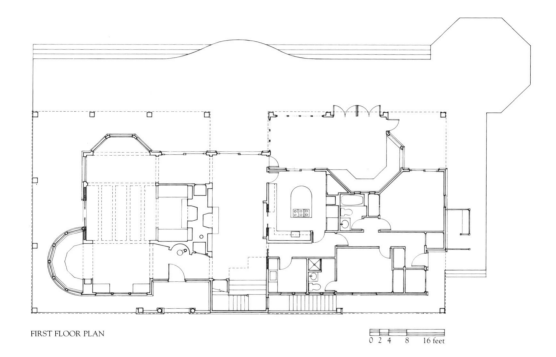

FIRST FLOOR PLAN

0 2 4 8 16 feet

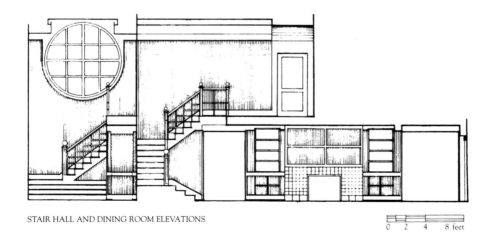

STAIR HALL AND DINING ROOM ELEVATIONS

0 2 4 8 feet

RESIDENCE AT CHILMARK
MARTHA'S VINEYARD, MASSACHUSETTS

Living room

Master bedroom

Stair

View from pool

Residence at Farm Neck
Martha's Vineyard, Massachusetts, 1980–83

Detail of porch

Southwest elevation

SECOND FLOOR PLAN

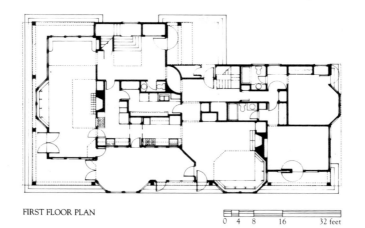

FIRST FLOOR PLAN

0 4 8   16   32 feet

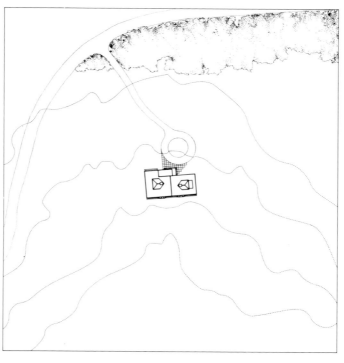

SITE PLAN

0 20 40   80   160 feet

RESIDENCE AT FARM NECK

MARTHA'S VINEYARD, MASSACHUSETTS

Master bedroom

Second-floor hallway

View into living room bay

Entrance

Approach to house

Garden elevation

Residence
East Hampton, New York, 1980–83

Entrance elevation

View of tower

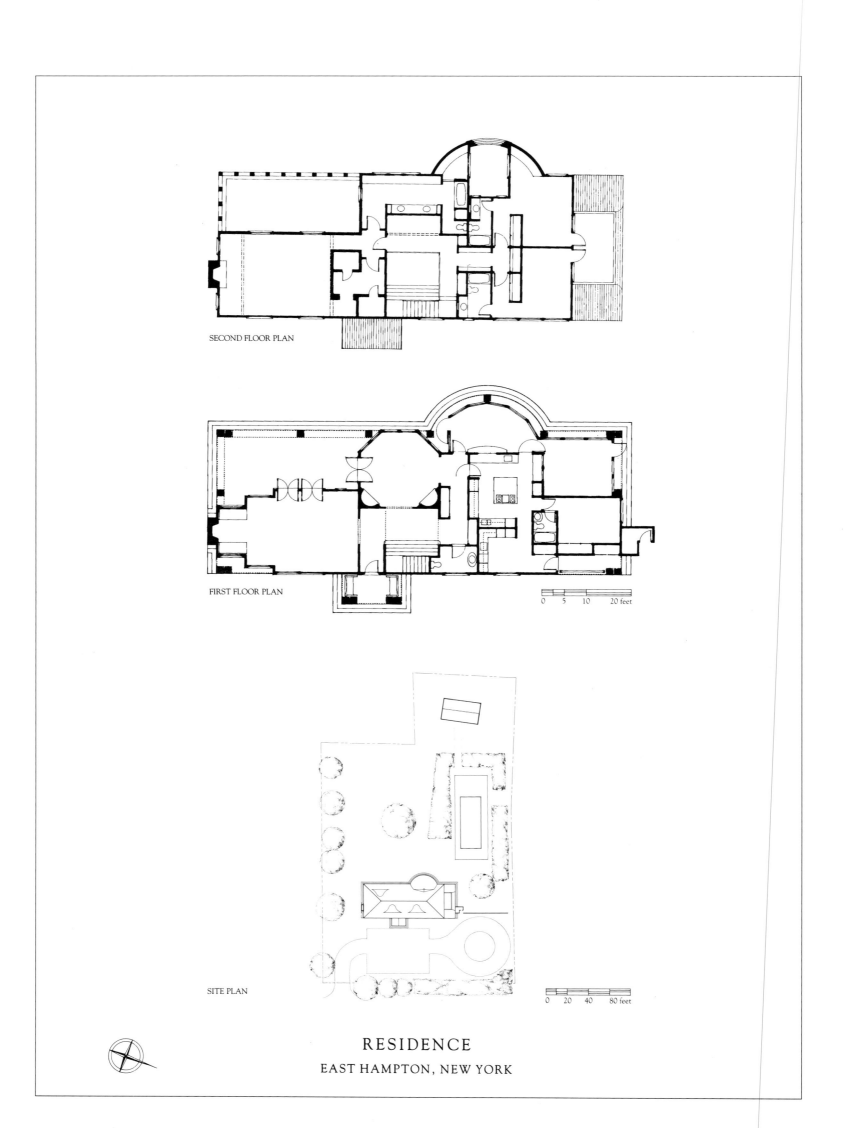

SECOND FLOOR PLAN

FIRST FLOOR PLAN

0   5   10   20 feet

SITE PLAN

0   20   40   80 feet

RESIDENCE

EAST HAMPTON, NEW YORK

SECTION THROUGH TOWER

ELEVATION OF TOWER

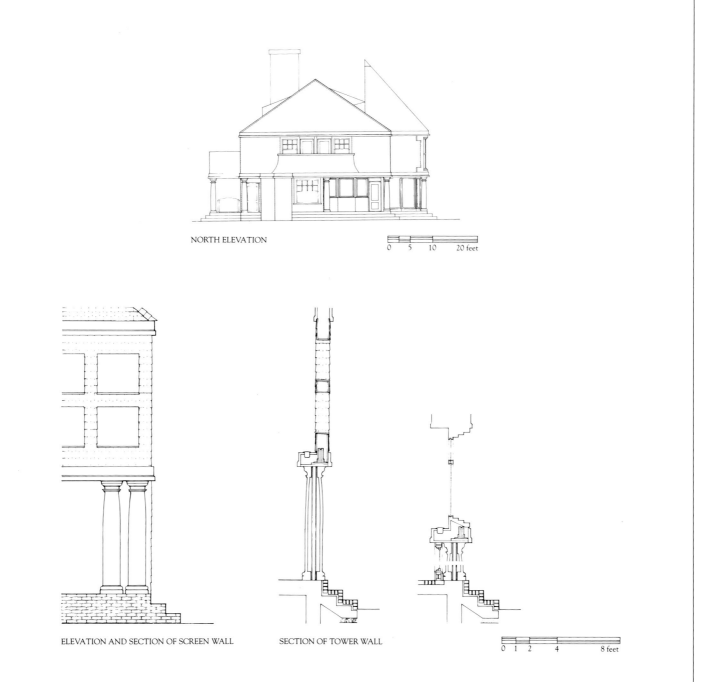

NORTH ELEVATION

0   5   10   20 feet

ELEVATION AND SECTION OF SCREEN WALL   SECTION OF TOWER WALL

0 1 2   4   8 feet

RESIDENCE

EAST HAMPTON, NEW YORK

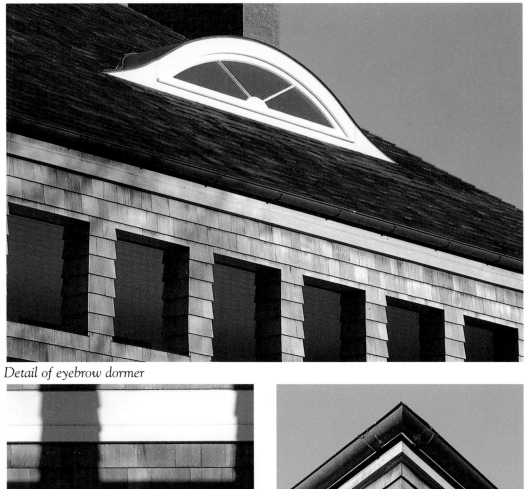

Detail of eyebrow dormer

Detail at porch

Detail of screen wall

View onto open porch

Stair

Living room

Dining room

View from southwest

Detail inside tower

Seaside elevation

Residence
Deal, New Jersey, 1982–84

Detail of window

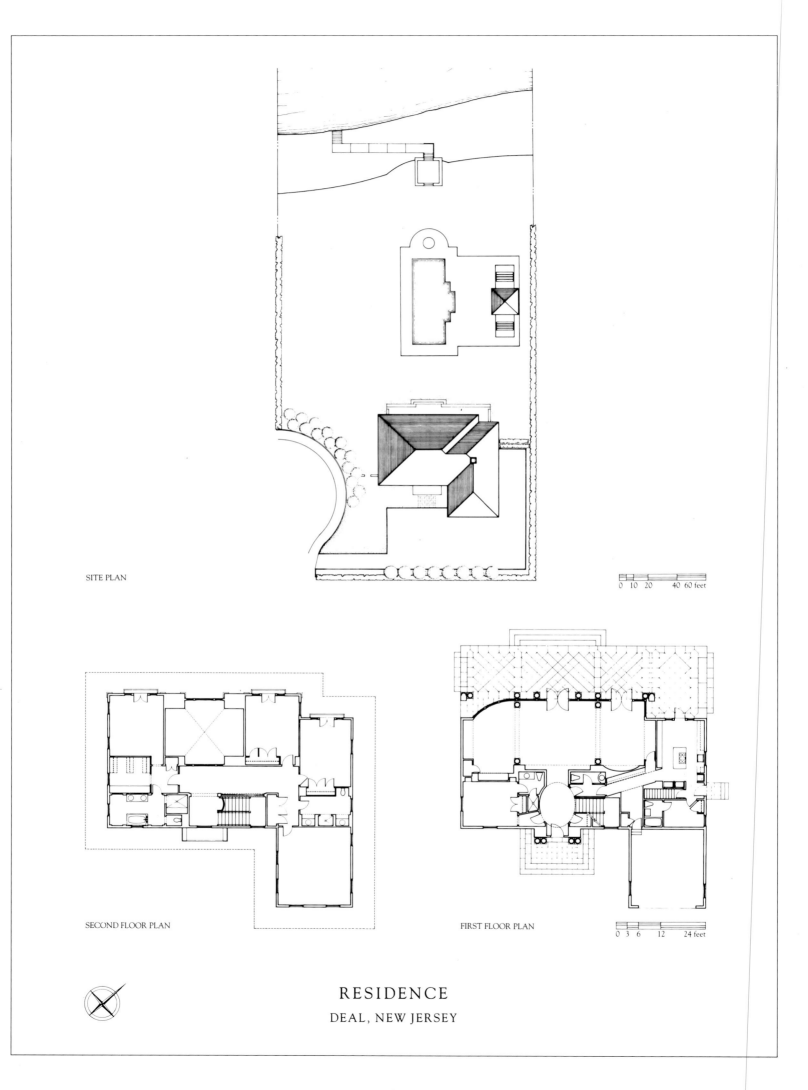

SITE PLAN

0 10 20 40 60 feet

SECOND FLOOR PLAN

FIRST FLOOR PLAN

0 3 6 12 24 feet

RESIDENCE

DEAL, NEW JERSEY

Entrance hall

Living room

View into living room

View from master bedroom

Seaside elevation

Residence
Hewlett Harbor, New York, 1984–88

Approach to house

Oblique view of entry

Entrance facade

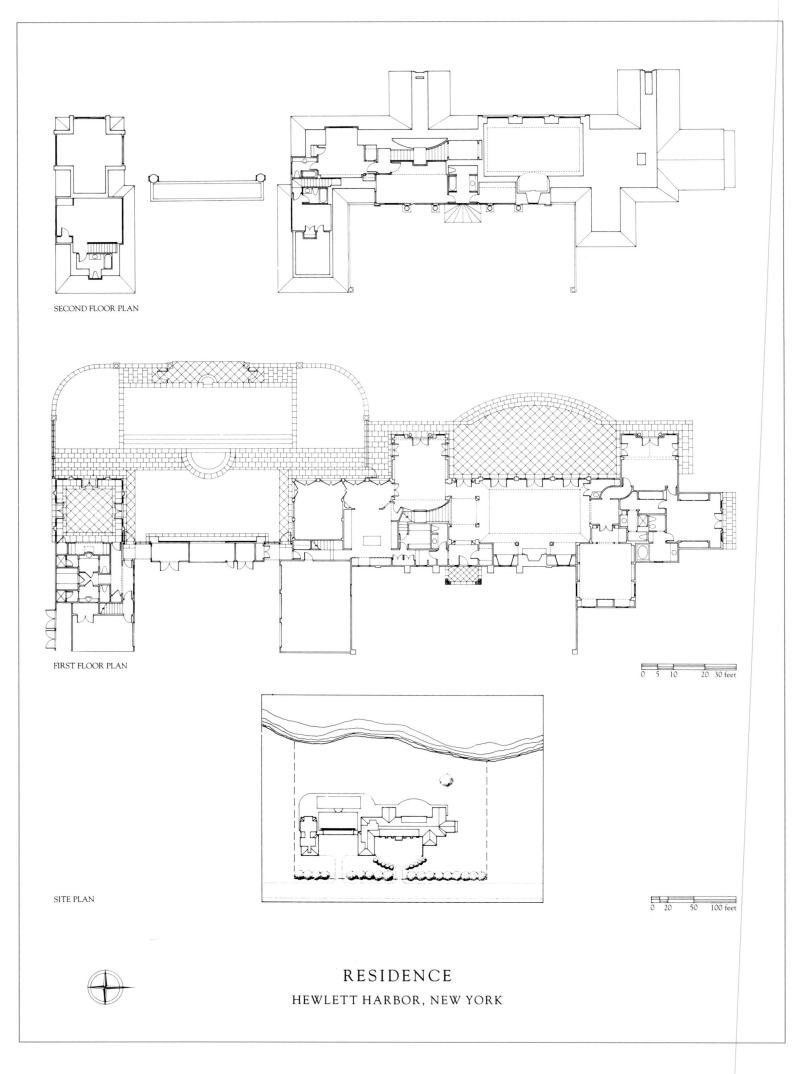

SECOND FLOOR PLAN

FIRST FLOOR PLAN

0 5 10 20 30 feet

SITE PLAN

0 20 50 100 feet

RESIDENCE

HEWLETT HARBOR, NEW YORK

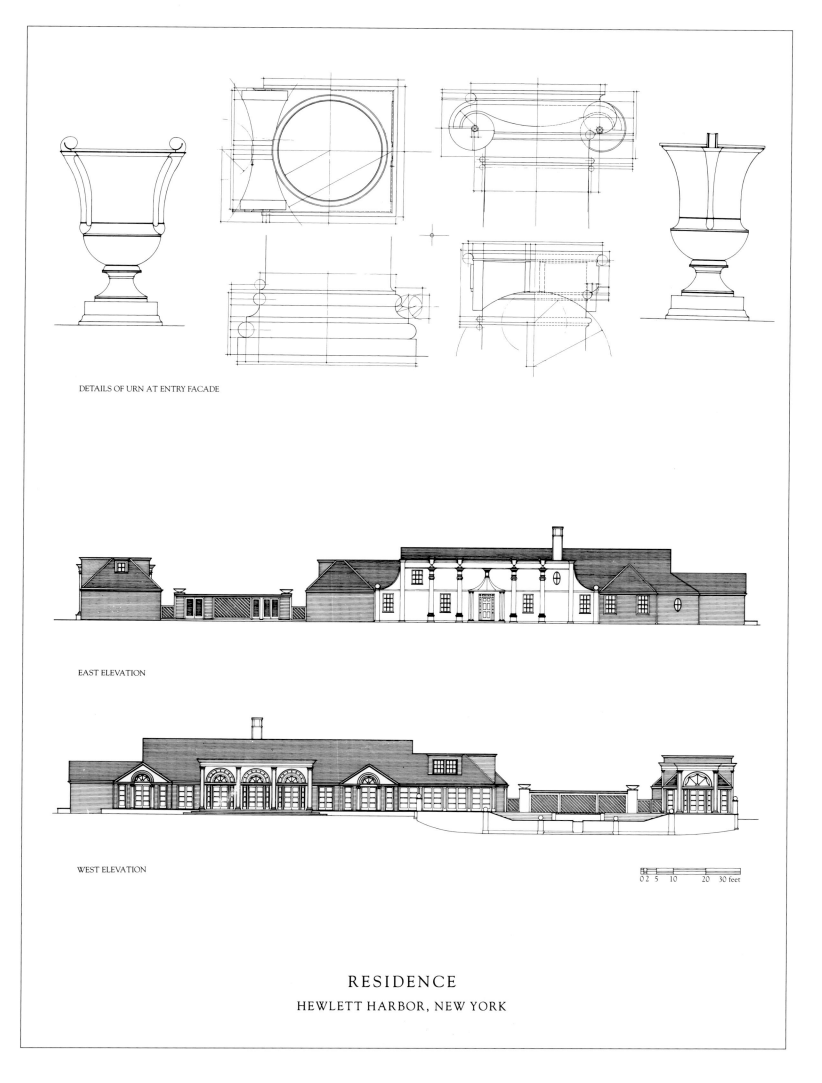

DETAILS OF URN AT ENTRY FACADE

EAST ELEVATION

WEST ELEVATION

0 2 5   10   20   30 feet

RESIDENCE
HEWLETT HARBOR, NEW YORK

Southwest corner

Northeast corner

Water elevation

View from entrance hall into living room

Living room

View from living room

Detail of living room

Dining room

Library

Detail of dining room

Seaside elevation

Residence
Marblehead, Massachusetts, 1984–87

View toward entrance

Detail at entrance

SECTION FACING SOUTHEAST

SECTION FACING SOUTHWEST

0 2 4   8   16 24 feet

SITE PLAN

0   20   40   80 120 feet

RESIDENCE
MARBLEHEAD, MASSACHUSETTS

122

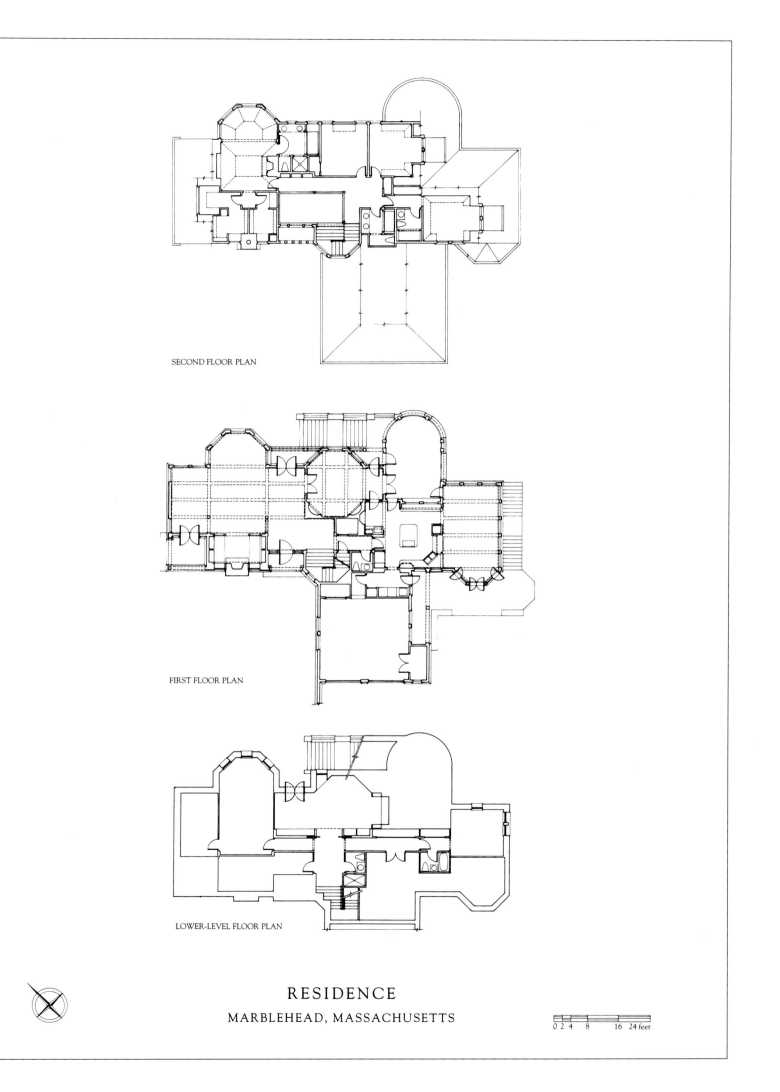

SECOND FLOOR PLAN

FIRST FLOOR PLAN

LOWER-LEVEL FLOOR PLAN

RESIDENCE

MARBLEHEAD, MASSACHUSETTS

0 2 4   8   16   24 feet

Detail of southwest court

View into stair tower

Sunstone
Quogue, New York, 1984–87

Bayside elevation

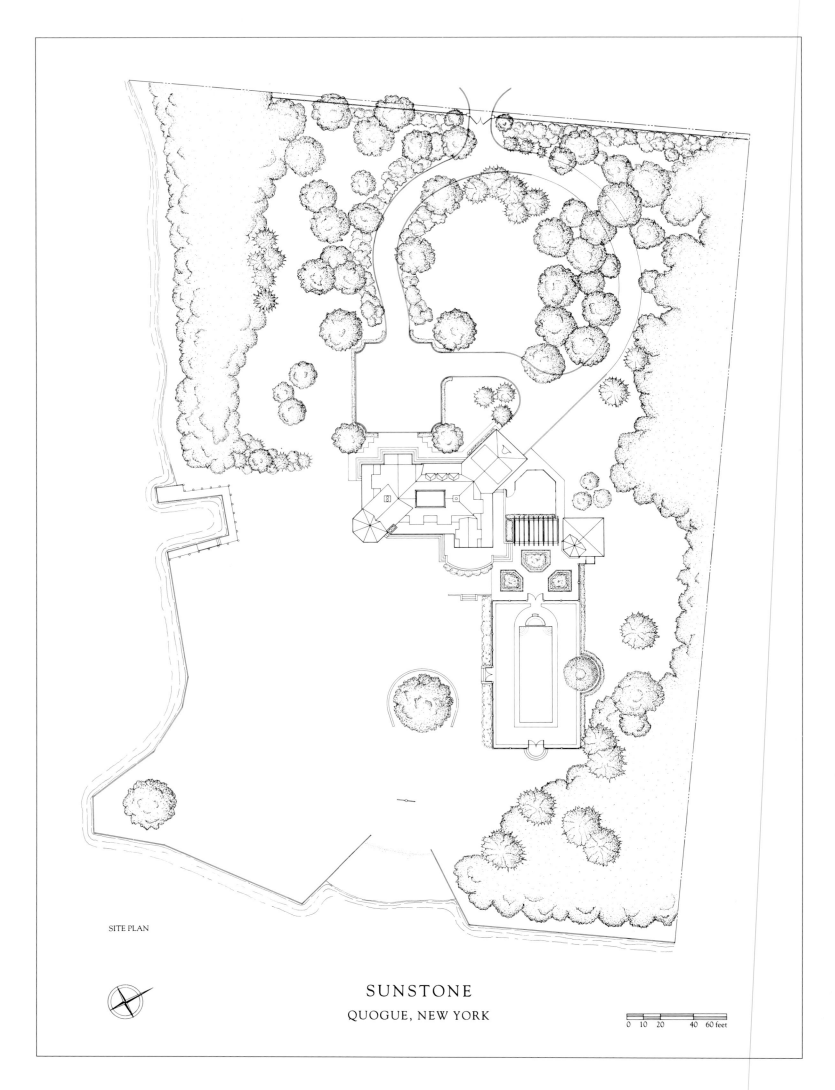

SITE PLAN

SUNSTONE

QUOGUE, NEW YORK

0 10 20   40   60 feet

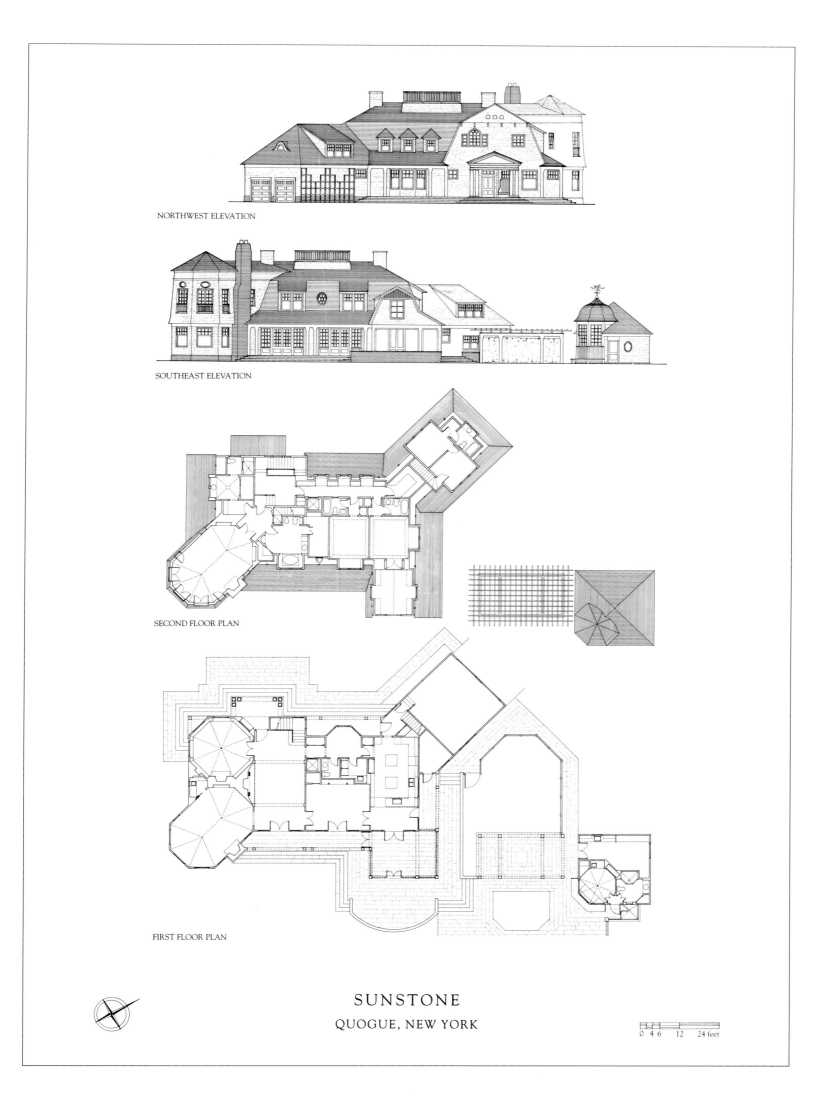

NORTHWEST ELEVATION

SOUTHEAST ELEVATION

SECOND FLOOR PLAN

FIRST FLOOR PLAN

SUNSTONE

QUOGUE, NEW YORK

0 4 6   12   24 feet

View from southwest

Entrance

View onto pool area

View of house across pool

Pergola and poolhouse

Living room

Entrance hall

Library

Kitchen

Master bedroom

Residence at Calf Creek
Water Mill, New York, 1984–87

Detail of library bay

Entrance

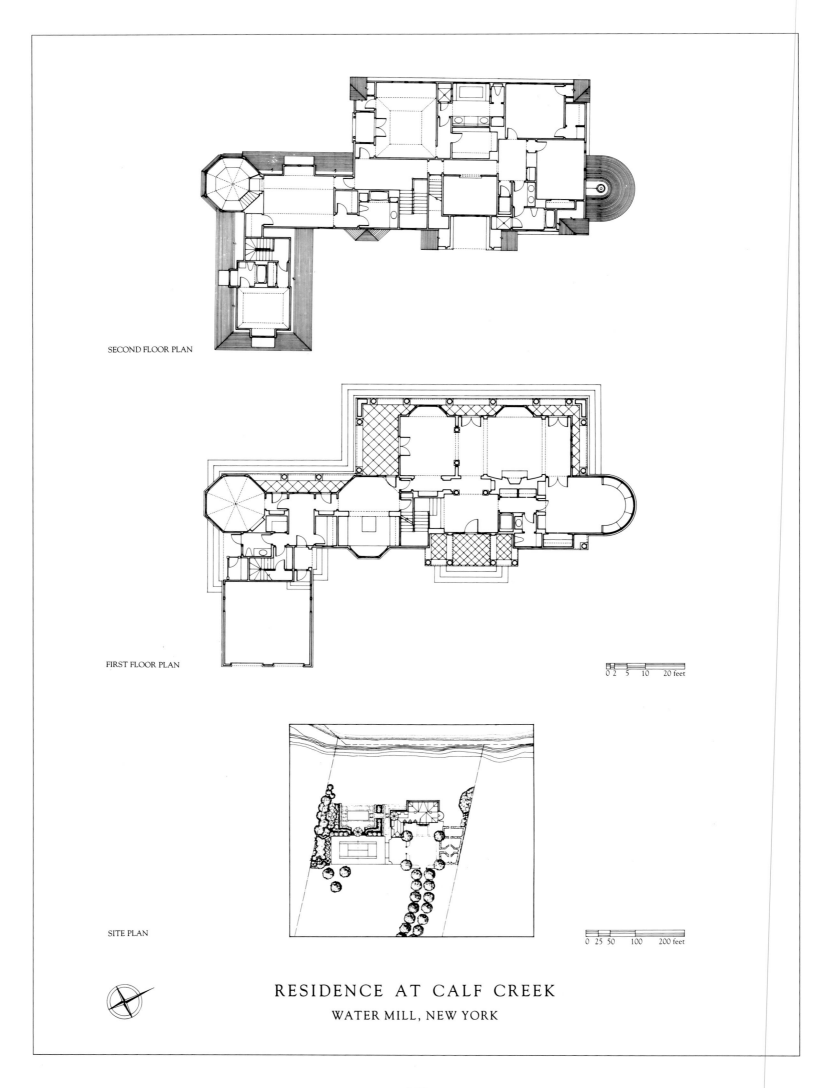

SECOND FLOOR PLAN

FIRST FLOOR PLAN

0 2 5 10 20 feet

SITE PLAN

0 25 50 100 200 feet

RESIDENCE AT CALF CREEK
WATER MILL, NEW YORK

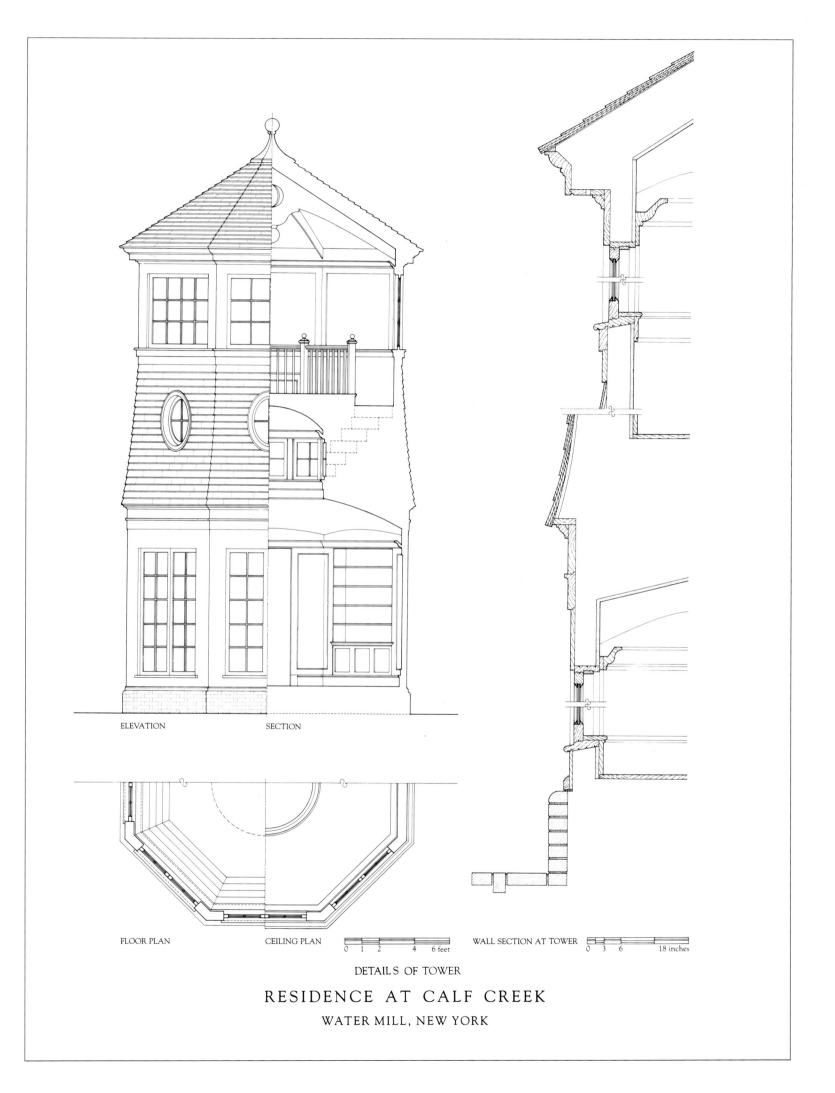

ELEVATION   SECTION

FLOOR PLAN   CEILING PLAN   0 1 2   4   6 feet   WALL SECTION AT TOWER   0   3   6   18 inches

DETAILS OF TOWER

RESIDENCE AT CALF CREEK

WATER MILL, NEW YORK

View of tower from pool

Pavilion

View from top of tower

Entrance hall

Living room

First floor of tower

Detail of dining room

West elevation from across Calf Creek

Entrance

Residence at Wilderness Point
Fishers Island, New York, 1986–89

Entrance elevation

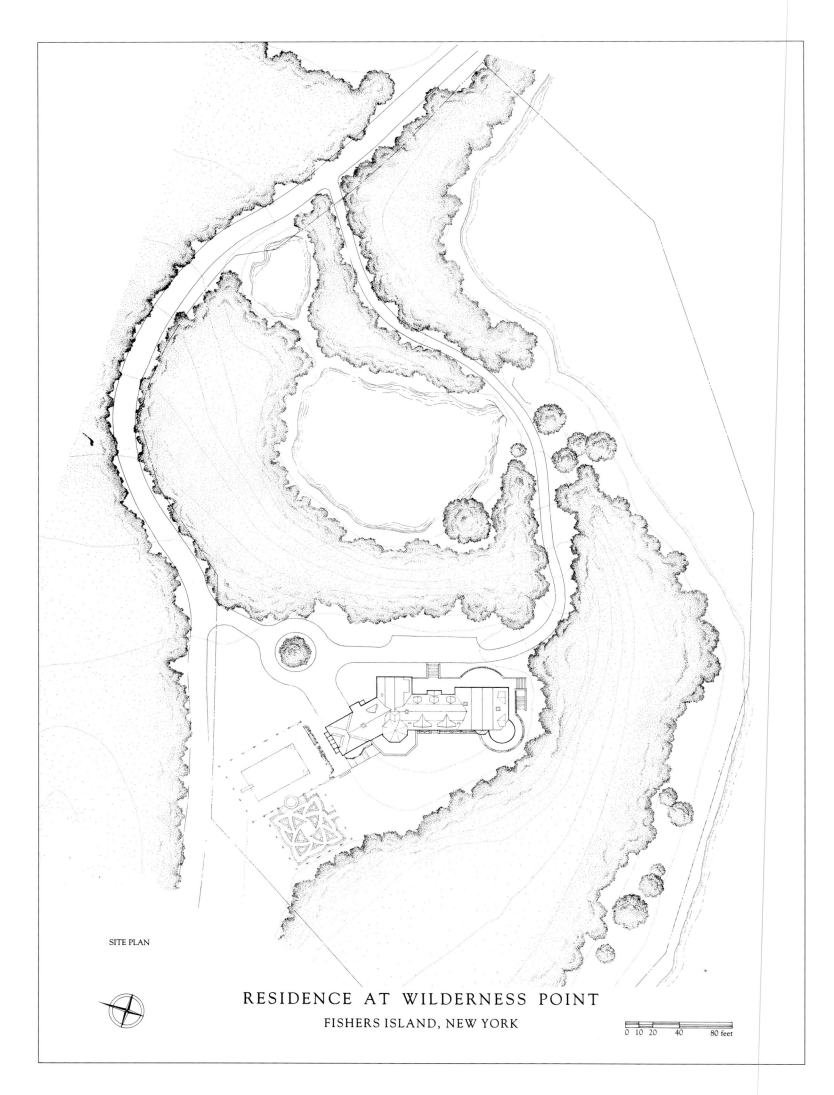

SITE PLAN

RESIDENCE AT WILDERNESS POINT

FISHERS ISLAND, NEW YORK

0 10 20   40   80 feet

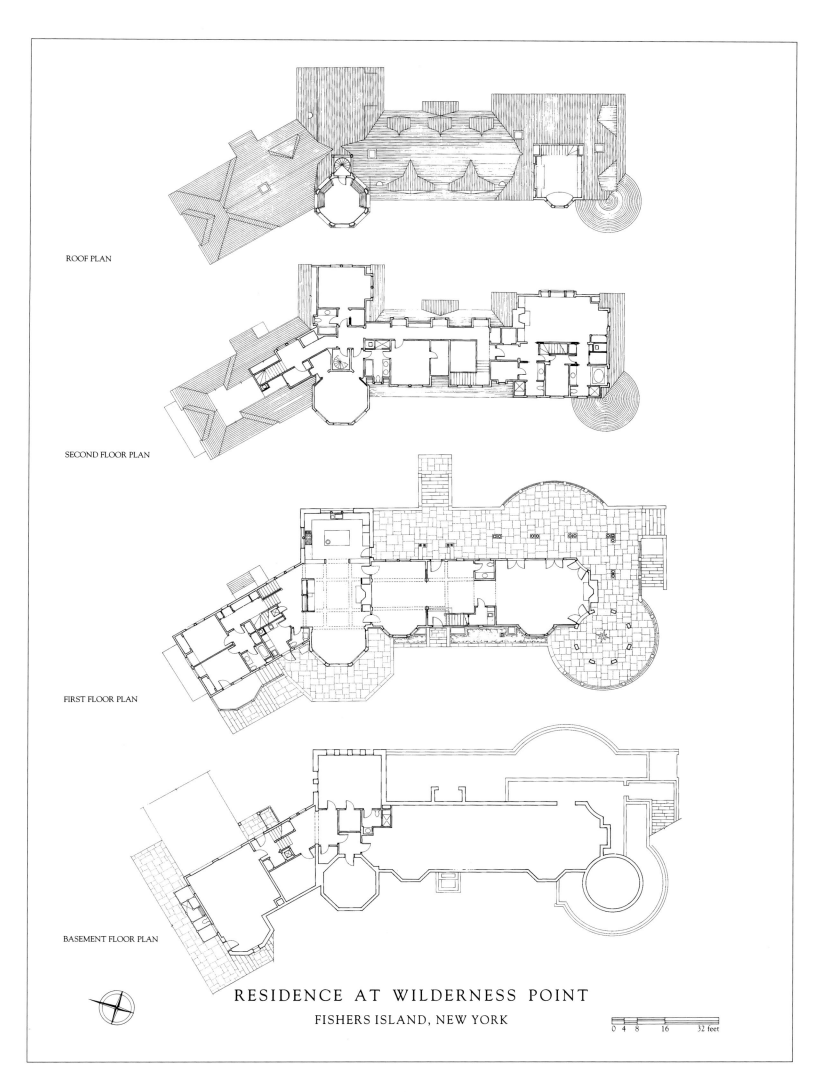

ROOF PLAN

SECOND FLOOR PLAN

FIRST FLOOR PLAN

BASEMENT FLOOR PLAN

RESIDENCE AT WILDERNESS POINT

FISHERS ISLAND, NEW YORK

0   4   8   16   32 feet

149

Entrance

Gazebo

Approach to house

Living room

Dining room

View into living room from entrance hall

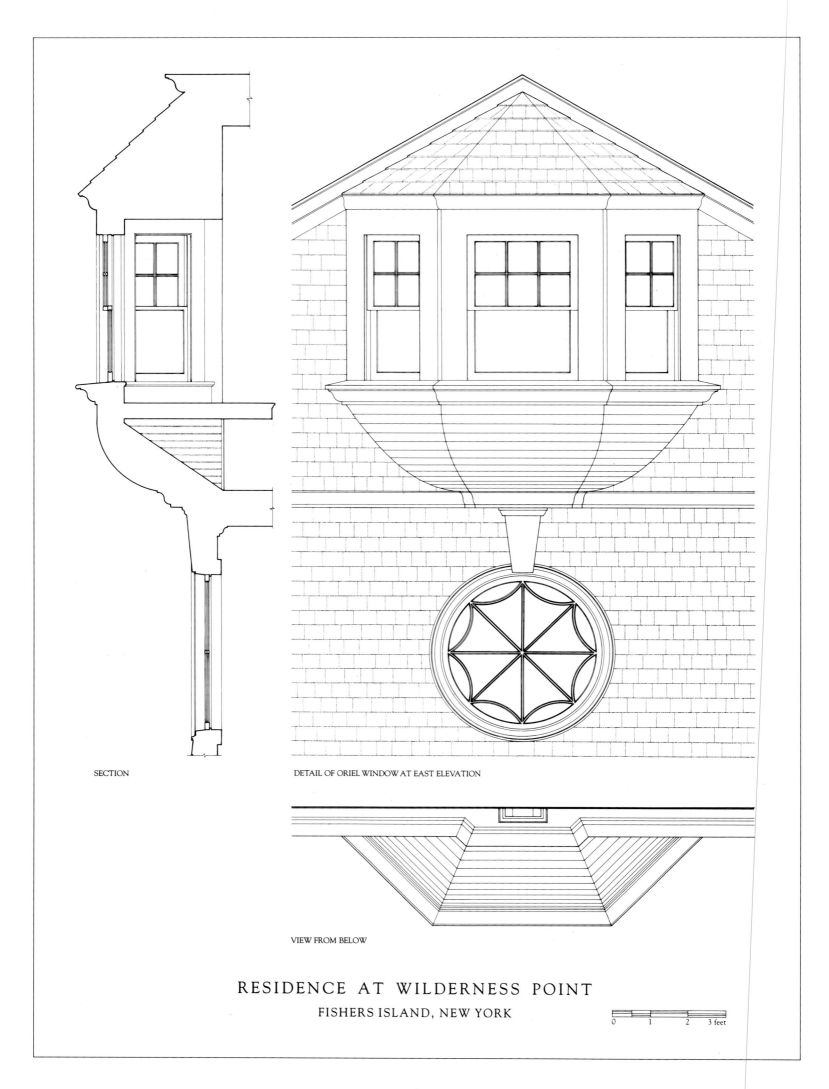

SECTION

DETAIL OF ORIEL WINDOW AT EAST ELEVATION

VIEW FROM BELOW

RESIDENCE AT WILDERNESS POINT

FISHERS ISLAND, NEW YORK

0   1   2   3 feet

Northeast corner

View from beach

Detail of tower

Residence

Elberon, New Jersey, 1985–89

Seaside elevation

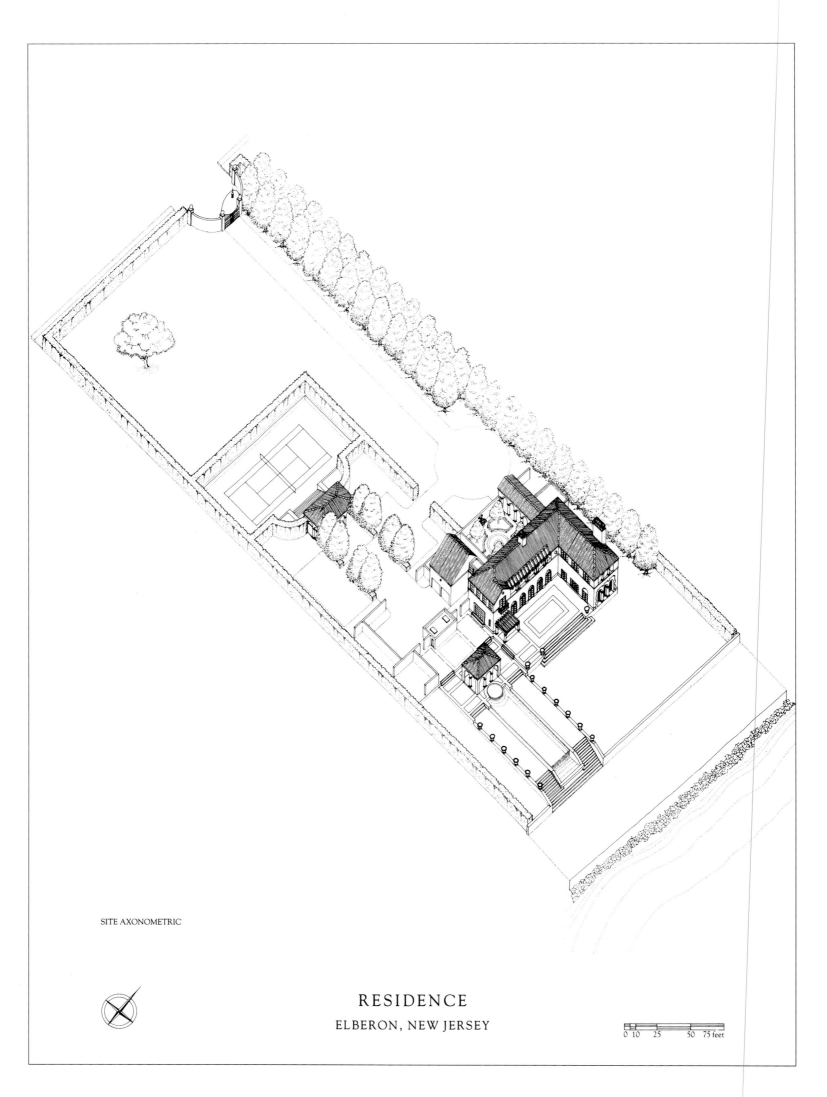

SITE AXONOMETRIC

RESIDENCE

ELBERON, NEW JERSEY

0 10 25 50 75 feet

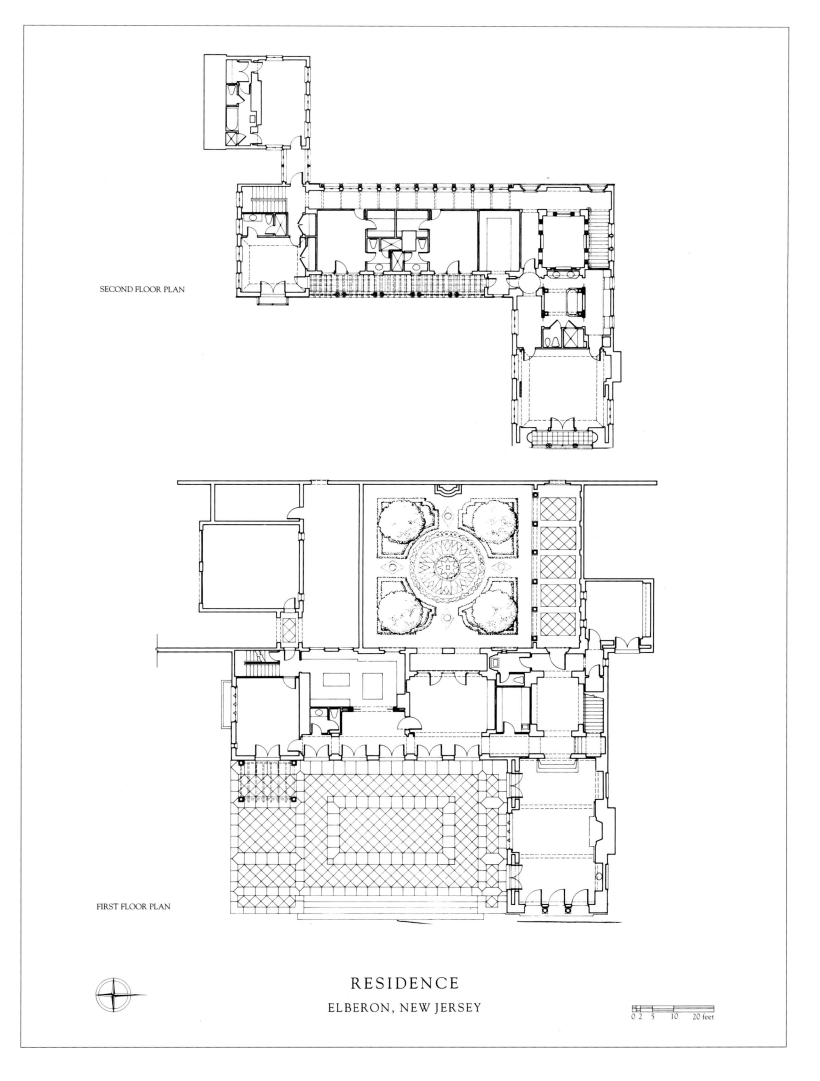

SECOND FLOOR PLAN

FIRST FLOOR PLAN

RESIDENCE

ELBERON, NEW JERSEY

0 2 5 10 20 feet

View of house from pool

View from pool to sea

Pebble garden

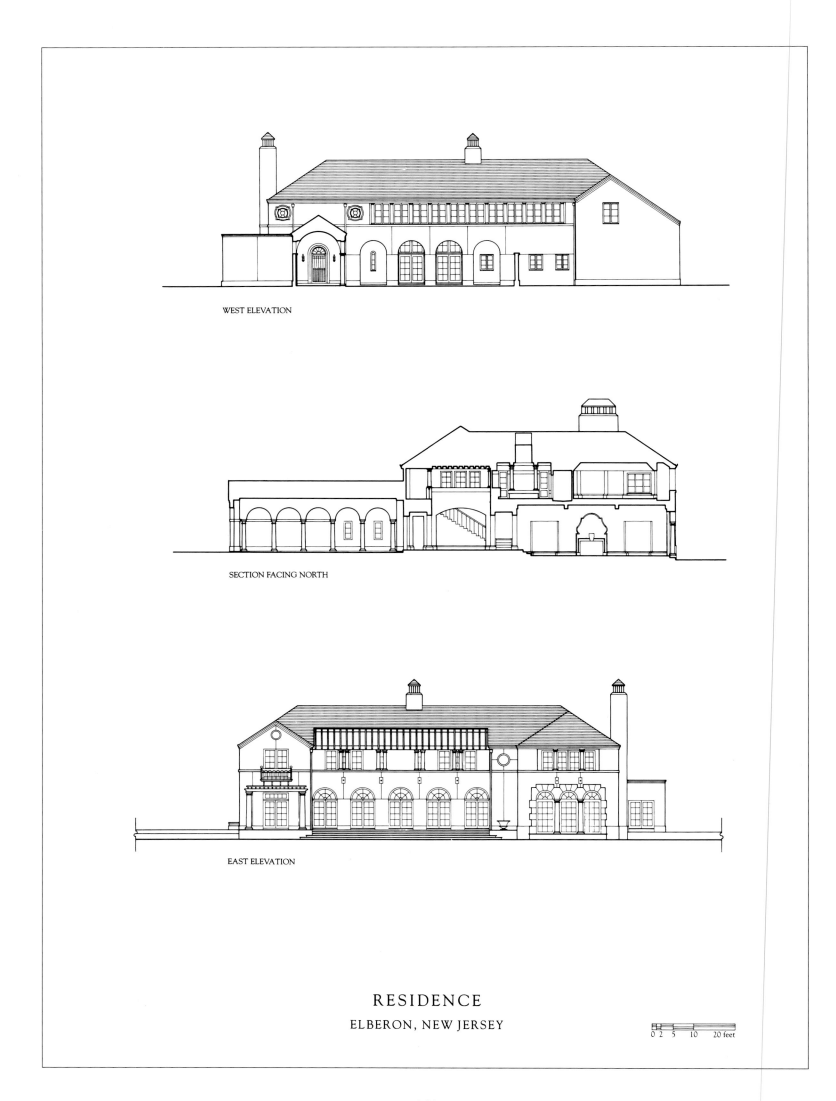

WEST ELEVATION

SECTION FACING NORTH

EAST ELEVATION

RESIDENCE

ELBERON, NEW JERSEY

0 2 5 10 20 feet

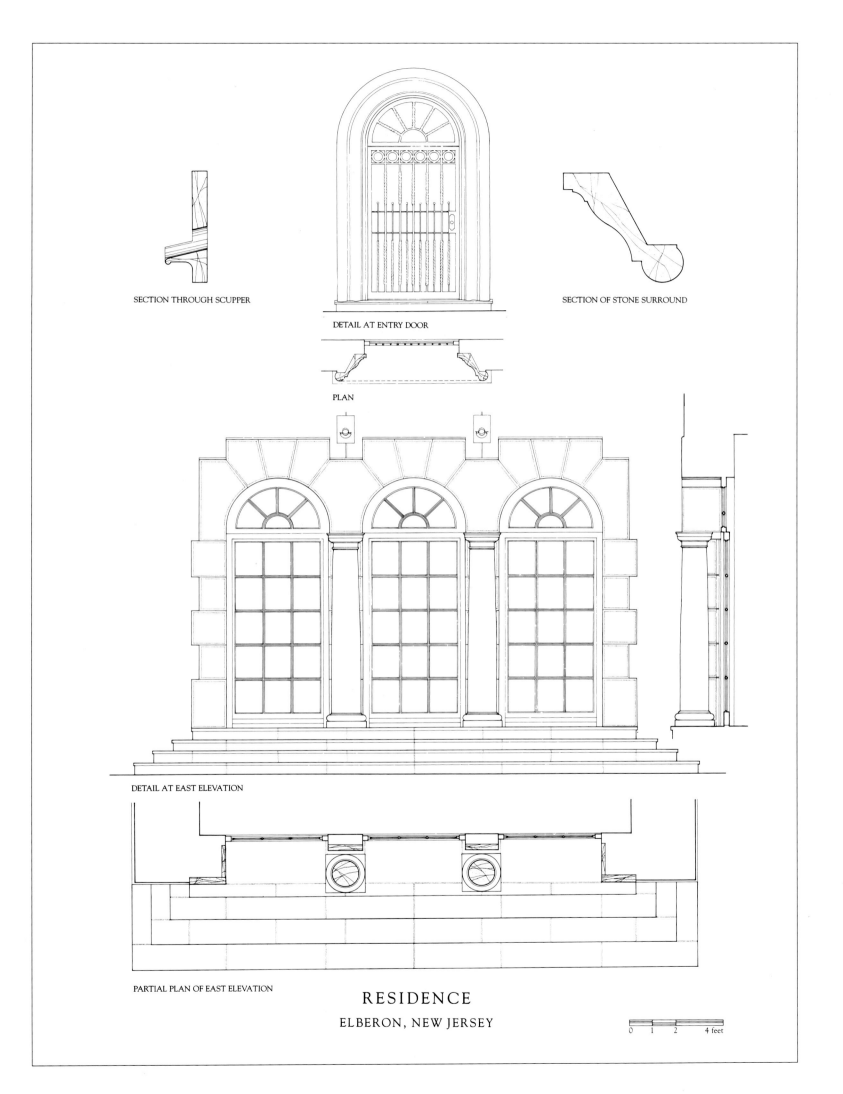

SECTION THROUGH SCUPPER

DETAIL AT ENTRY DOOR

SECTION OF STONE SURROUND

PLAN

DETAIL AT EAST ELEVATION

PARTIAL PLAN OF EAST ELEVATION

RESIDENCE

ELBERON, NEW JERSEY

0   1   2   4 feet

View of pebble garden from dining room

Living room

East loggia

Master dressing room

Entrance hall

Entrance

Villa in New Jersey
1983–89

South elevation

WILLIAM THEODORE GEORGIS 1985 DEL.

Arché

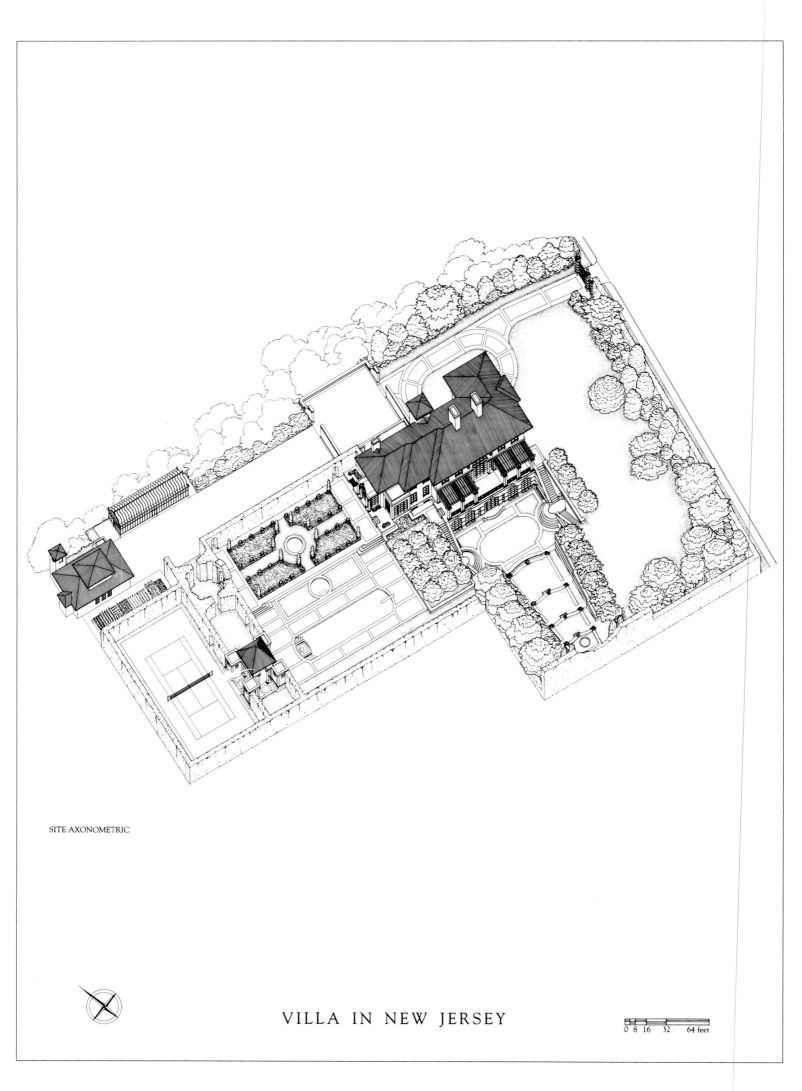

SITE AXONOMETRIC

VILLA IN NEW JERSEY

0 8 16   32   64 feet

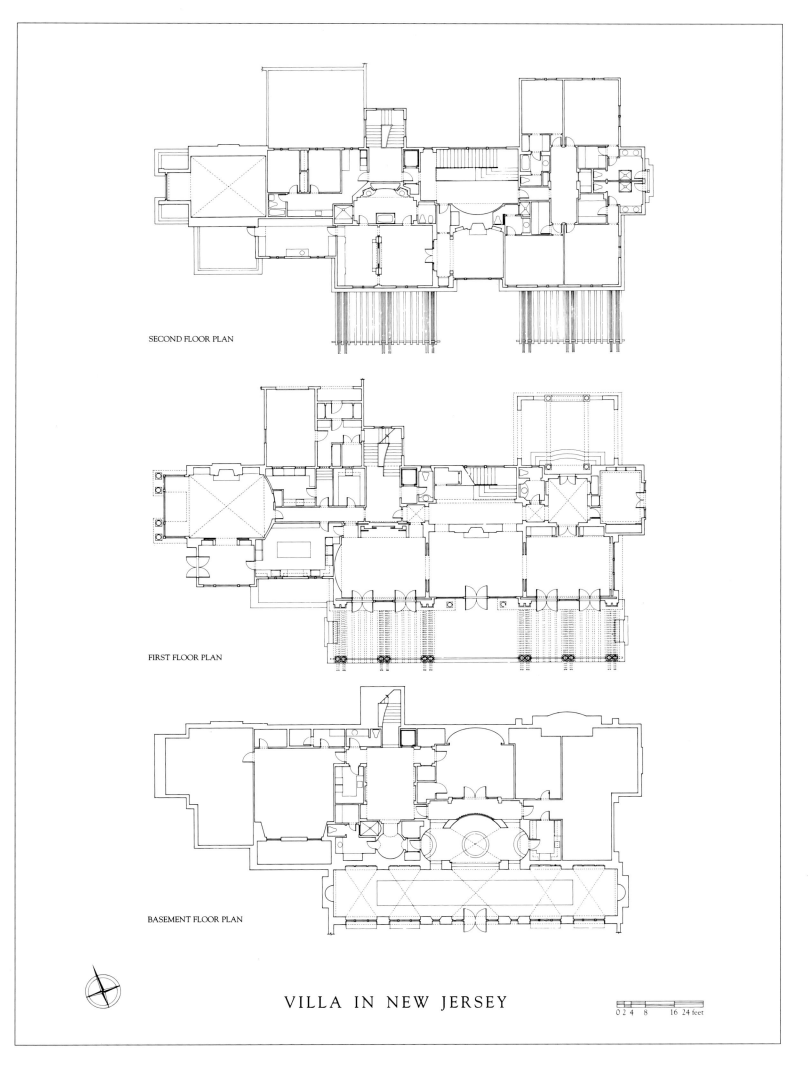

SECOND FLOOR PLAN

FIRST FLOOR PLAN

BASEMENT FLOOR PLAN

VILLA IN NEW JERSEY

0 2 4 8   16 24 feet

Entrance

East elevation

Entrance gates

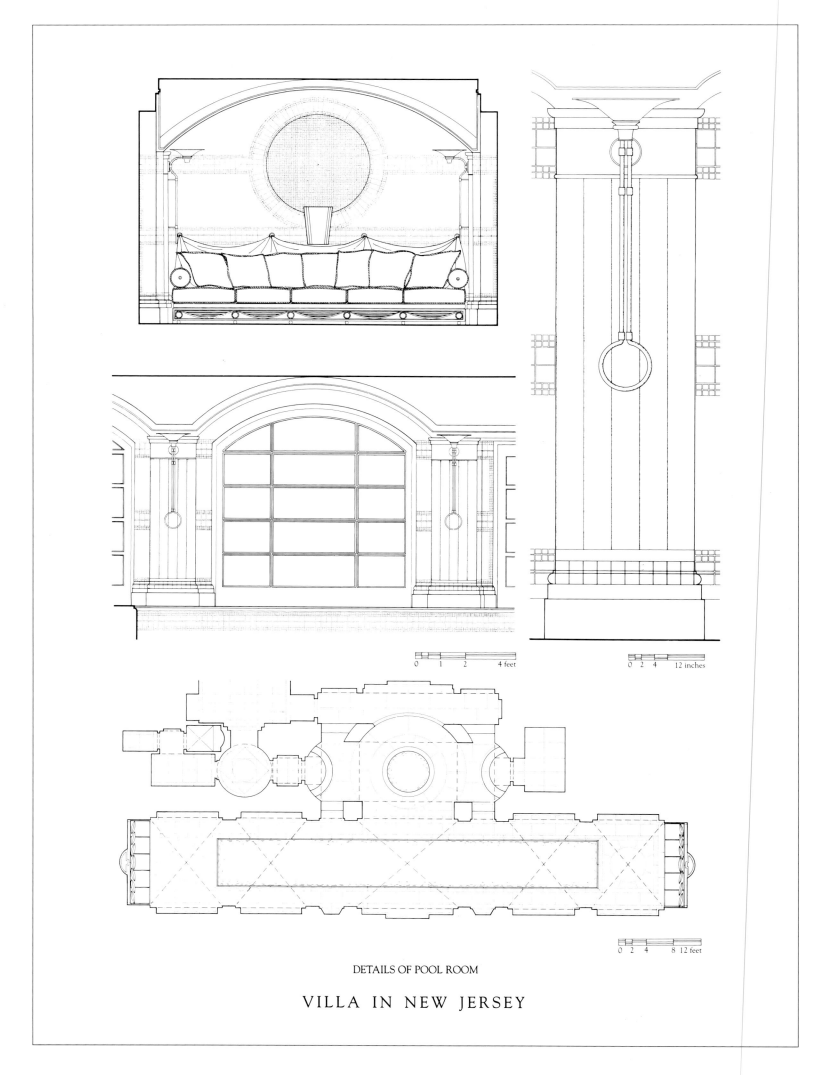

0 1 2   4 feet

0 2 4   12 inches

0 2 4   8 12 feet

DETAILS OF POOL ROOM

VILLA IN NEW JERSEY

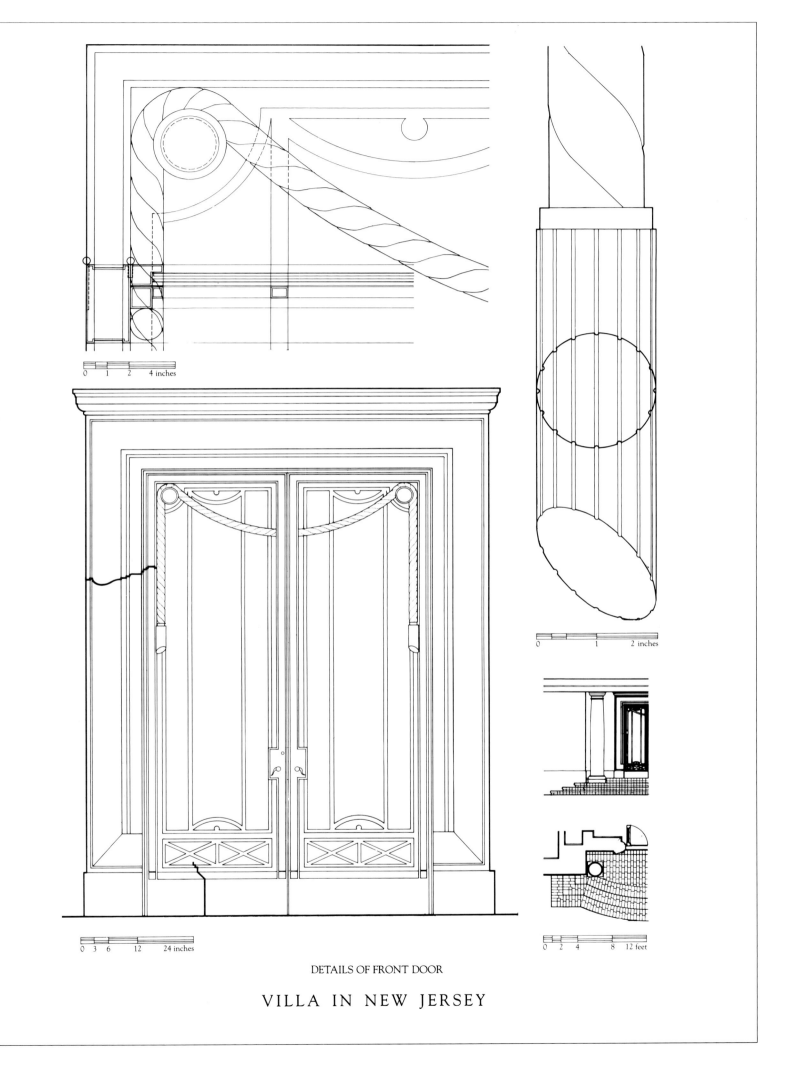

0 1 2 4 inches

0   1   2 inches

0   3   6   12   24 inches

0   2   4   8   12 feet

DETAILS OF FRONT DOOR

VILLA IN NEW JERSEY

South elevation

View into sunken garden from south terrace

View across flower garden toward pool pavilion

West elevation from garden

179

DETAILS OF ENTRANCE GATE

VILLA IN NEW JERSEY

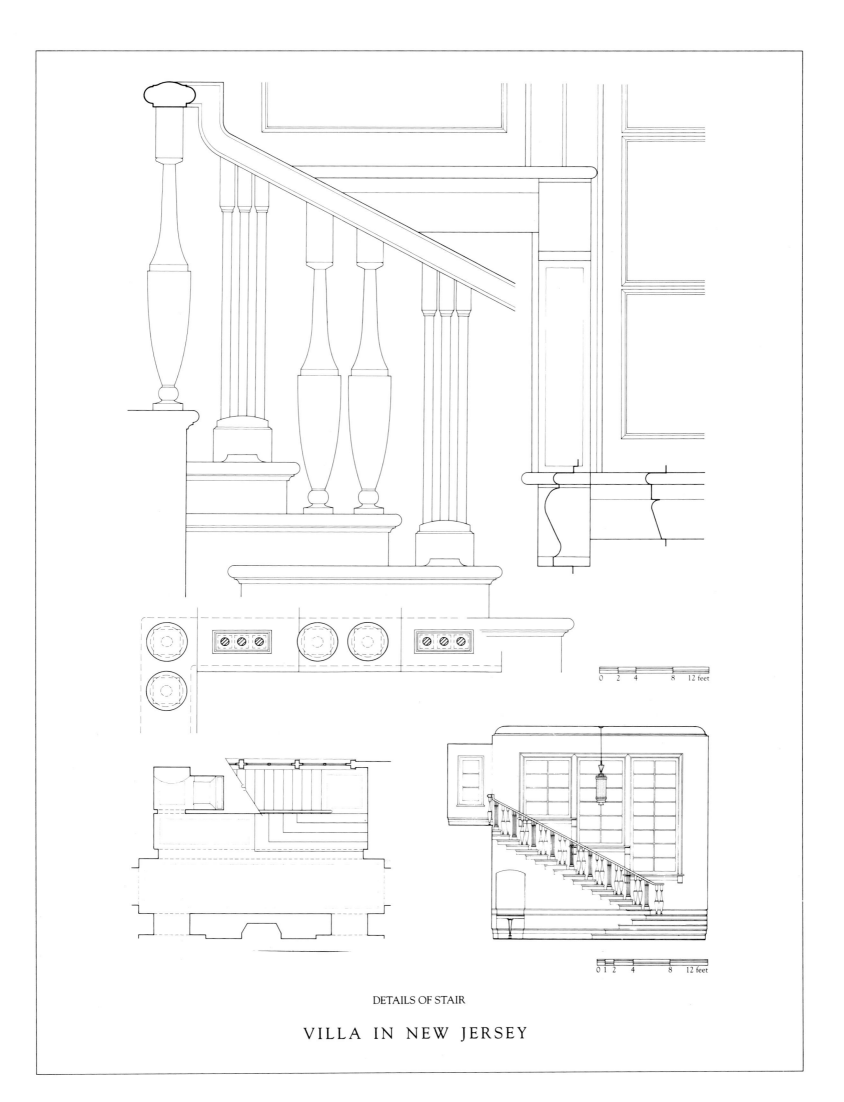

DETAILS OF STAIR

VILLA IN NEW JERSEY

Family room

Card room

Living room

Back stair

Entrance hall

Phone room

Pool changing room

Dressing room

Indoor pool

Pool pavilion

South elevation

HOUSES
IN THE MOUNTAINS

Sky View
Aspen, Colorado, 1987–90

South elevation

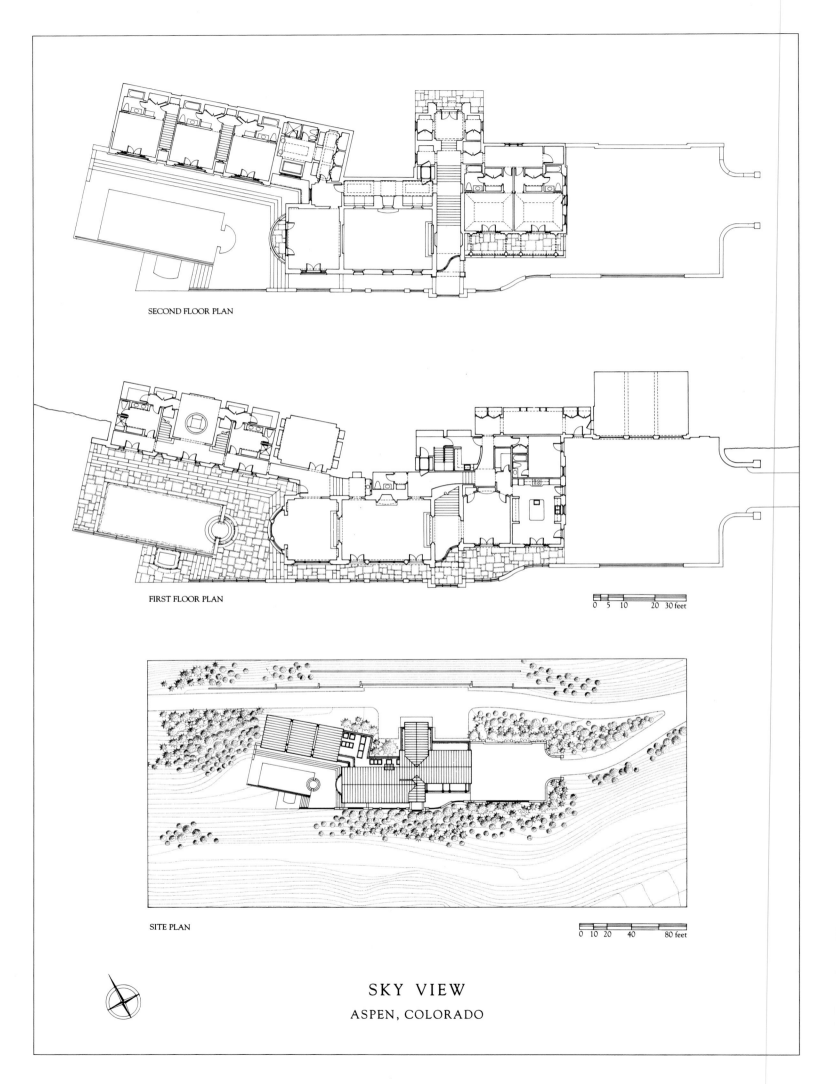

SECOND FLOOR PLAN

FIRST FLOOR PLAN

0 5 10   20 30 feet

SITE PLAN

0 10 20   40   80 feet

SKY VIEW

ASPEN, COLORADO

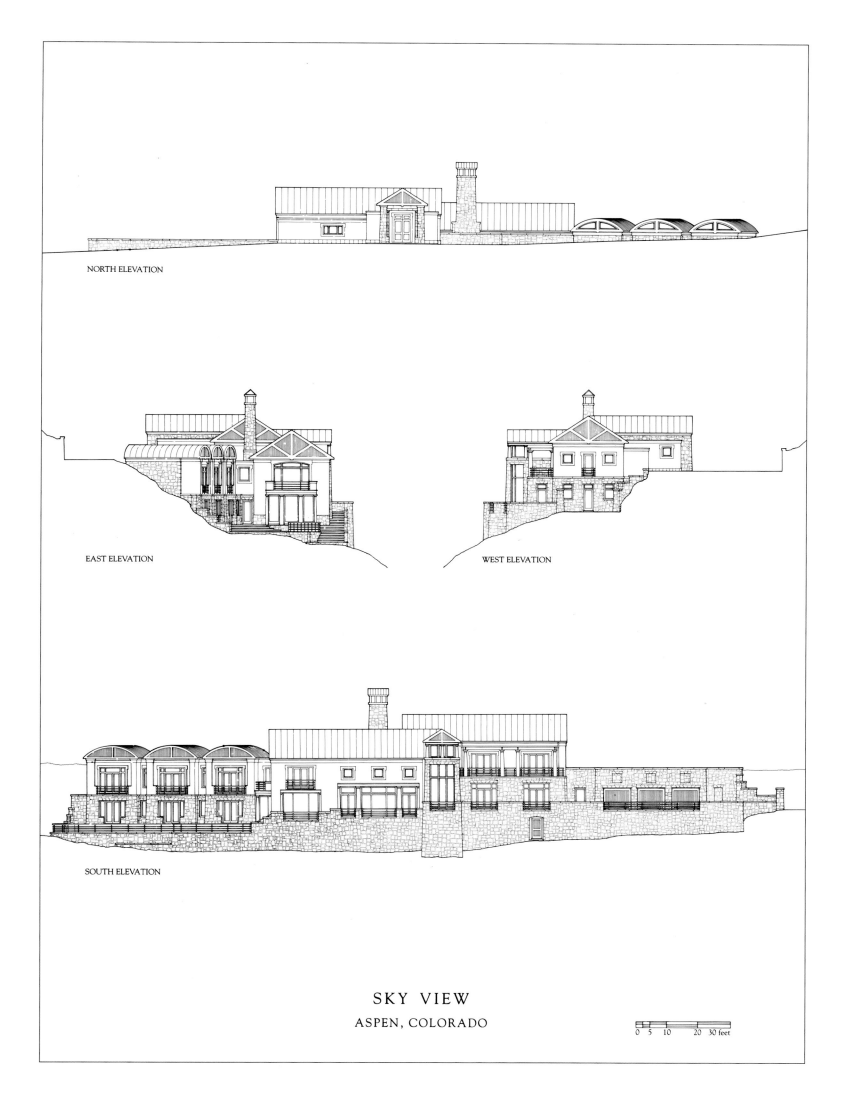

NORTH ELEVATION

EAST ELEVATION

WEST ELEVATION

SOUTH ELEVATION

SKY VIEW

ASPEN, COLORADO

0 5 10   20 30 feet

Spruce Lodge
Old Snowmass, Colorado, 1987–91

Southwest elevation

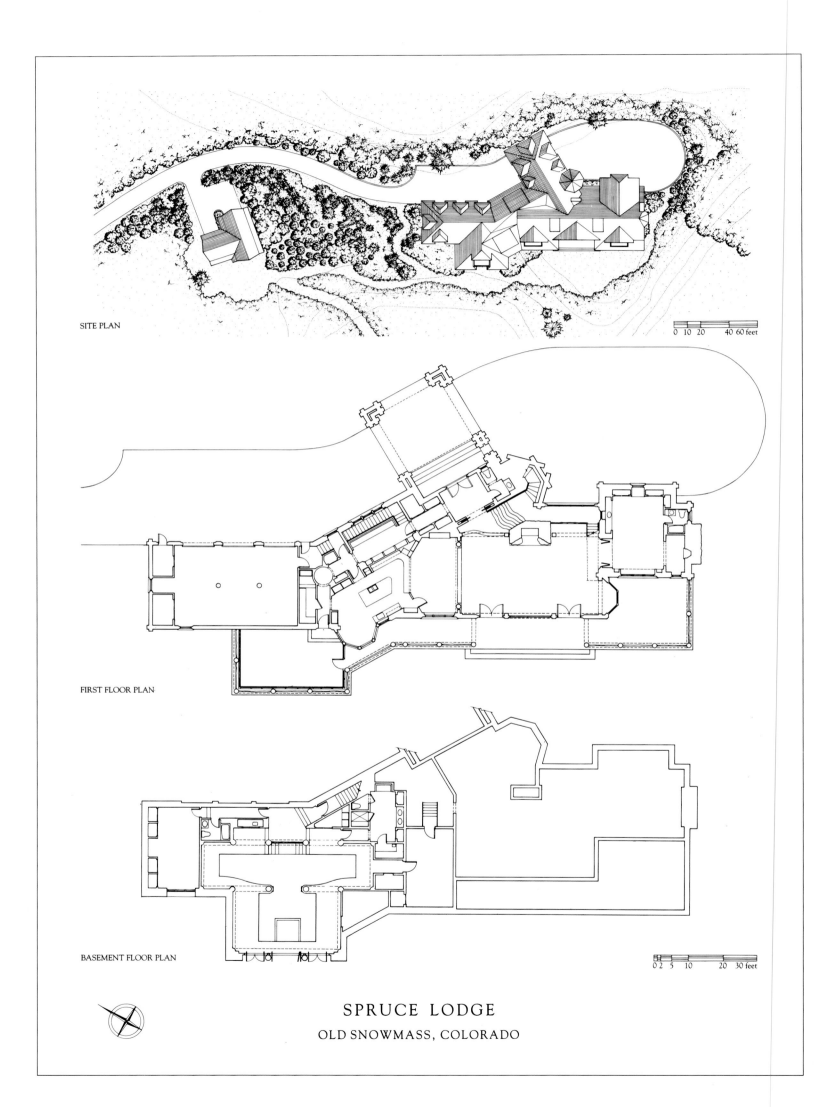

SITE PLAN

0 10 20   40 60 feet

FIRST FLOOR PLAN

BASEMENT FLOOR PLAN

0 2 5   10   20 30 feet

SPRUCE LODGE
OLD SNOWMASS, COLORADO

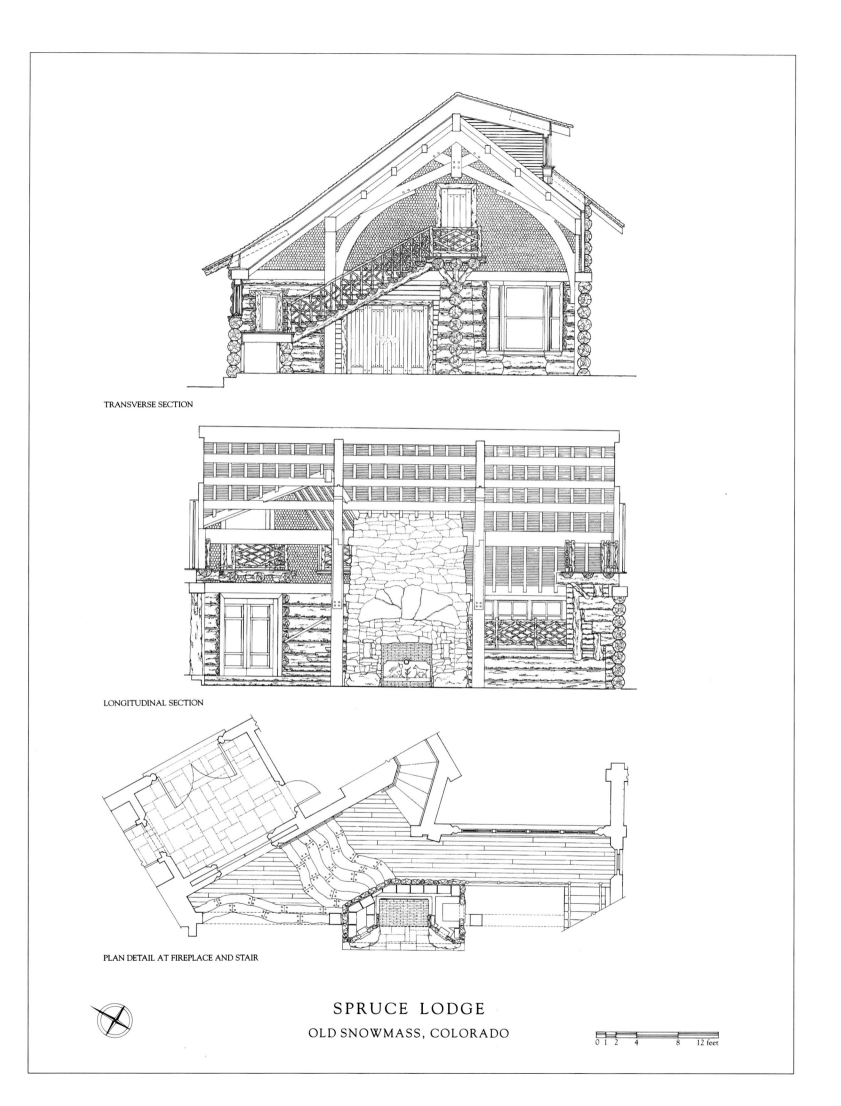

TRANSVERSE SECTION

LONGITUDINAL SECTION

PLAN DETAIL AT FIREPLACE AND STAIR

SPRUCE LODGE

OLD SNOWMASS, COLORADO

0 1 2   4   8   12 feet

HOUSES IN TOWN

Residence
Brooklyn, New York, 1983–86

Street facade

View from street

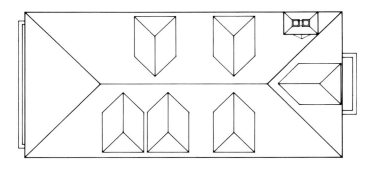

ROOF PLAN

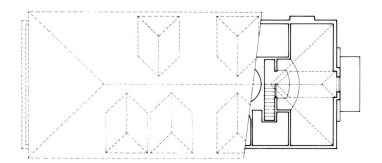

ATTIC FLOOR PLAN

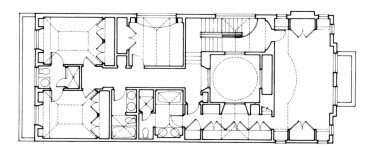

SECOND FLOOR PLAN

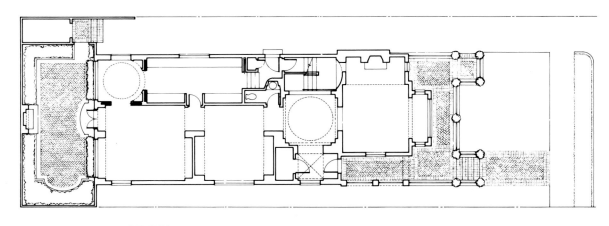

FIRST FLOOR PLAN

RESIDENCE

BROOKLYN, NEW YORK

0   5   10   20 feet

EAST ELEVATION

TRANSVERSE SECTION AT LIVING ROOM AND MASTER BEDROOM

LONGITUDINAL SECTION

WEST ELEVATION

TRANSVERSE SECTION AT ENTRANCE HALL

RESIDENCE

BROOKLYN, NEW YORK

0   5   10   20 feet

View into garden

Detail of street facade

Gateway into garden

View from west

Residence on Russian Hill
San Francisco, California, 1985–89

Entrance

View from east

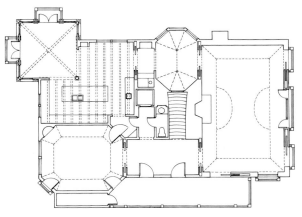

THIRD FLOOR PLAN

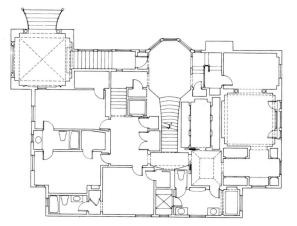

SECOND FLOOR PLAN

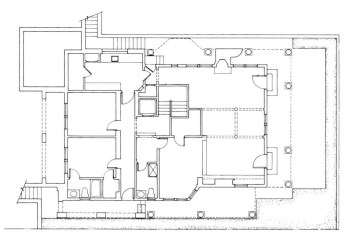

FIRST FLOOR PLAN

0 2 5   10   20 feet

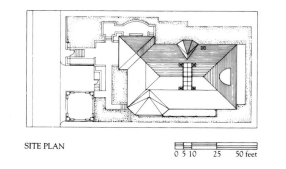

SITE PLAN

0 5 10   25   50 feet

RESIDENCE ON RUSSIAN HILL
SAN FRANCISCO, CALIFORNIA

LONGITUDINAL SECTION LOOKING SOUTH

TRANSVERSE SECTION LOOKING EAST

LONGITUDINAL SECTION LOOKING NORTH

RESIDENCE ON RUSSIAN HILL

SAN FRANCISCO, CALIFORNIA

0 2 4   8   16   24 feet

211

Principal stair

Living room

Family room

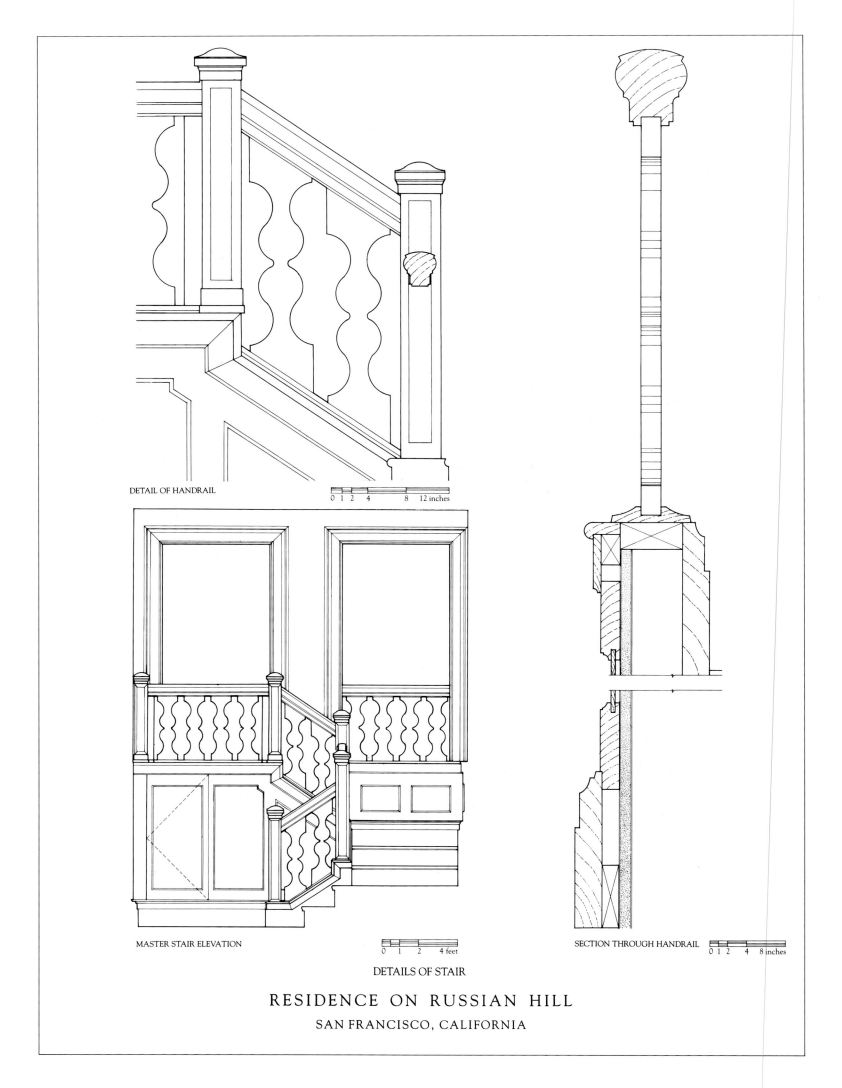

DETAIL OF HANDRAIL

0 1 2 4 8 12 inches

MASTER STAIR ELEVATION

0 1 2 4 feet

SECTION THROUGH HANDRAIL

0 1 2 4 8 inches

DETAILS OF STAIR

RESIDENCE ON RUSSIAN HILL
SAN FRANCISCO, CALIFORNIA

View of stair to master bedroom

Residence at North York
Ontario, Canada, 1988–

Entrance elevation

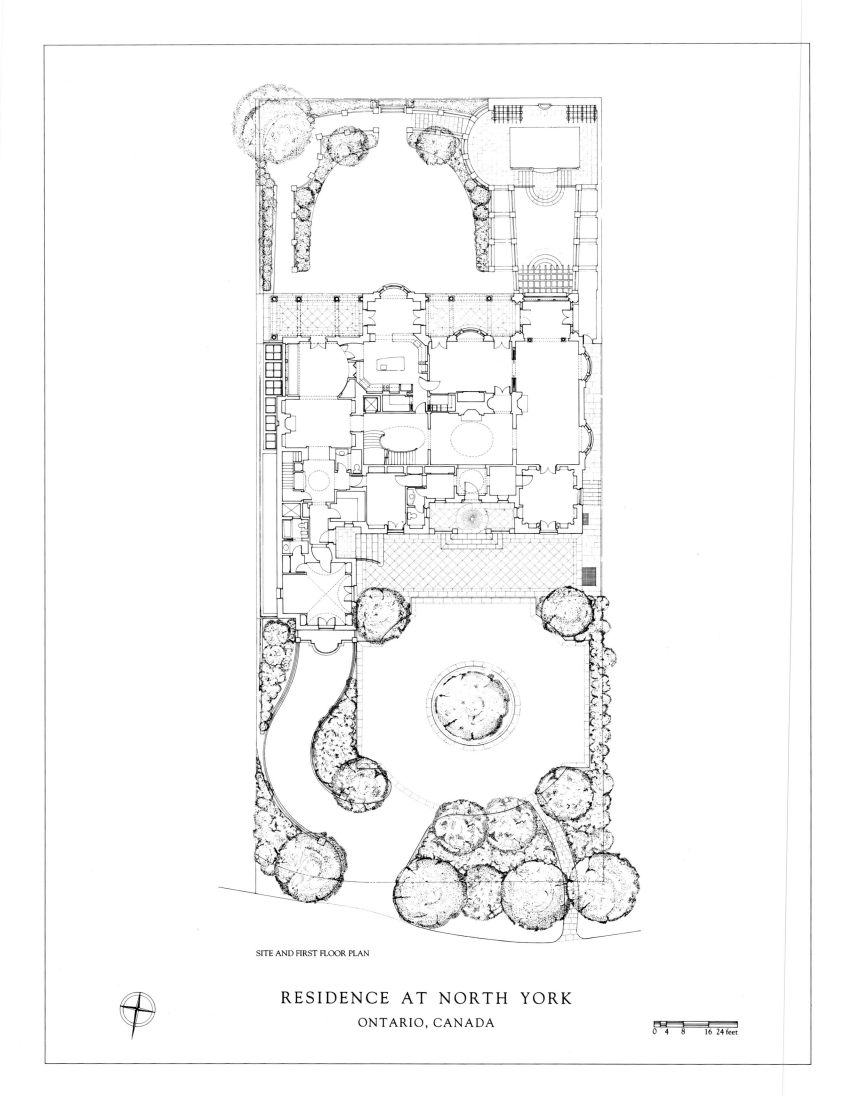

SITE AND FIRST FLOOR PLAN

RESIDENCE AT NORTH YORK

ONTARIO, CANADA

0 4 8 16 24 feet

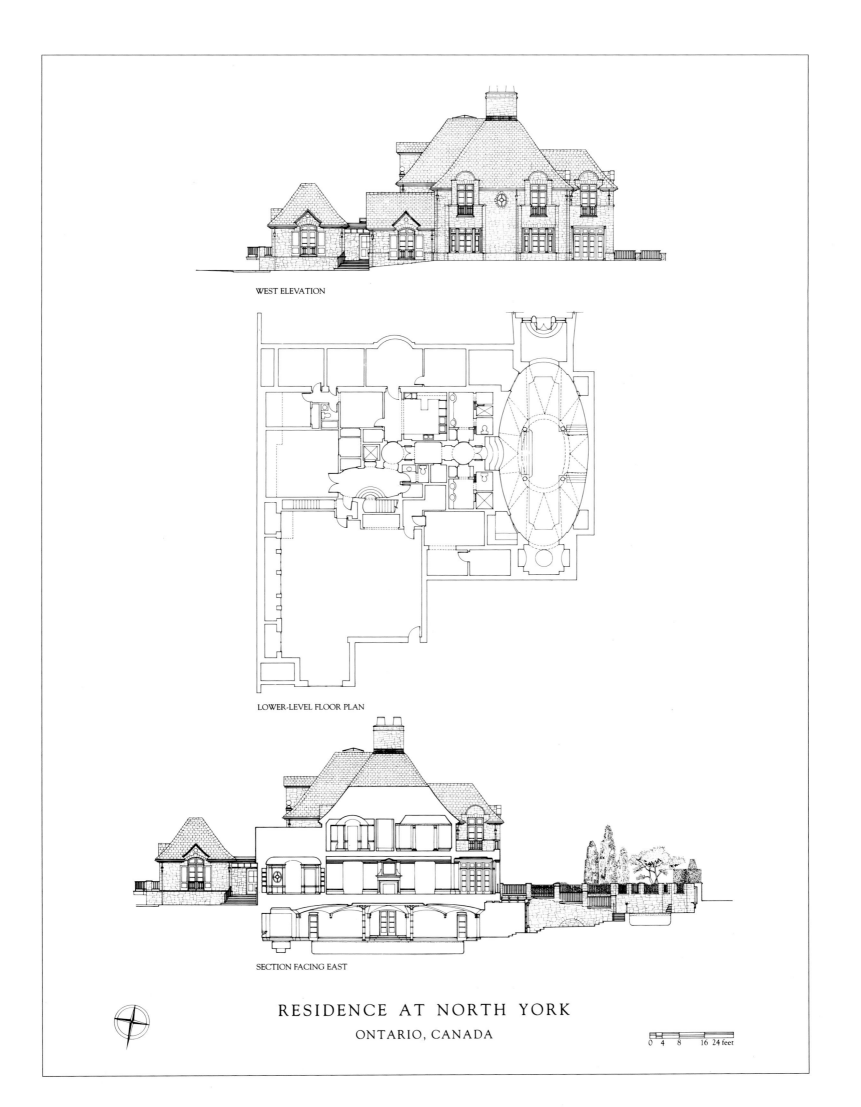

WEST ELEVATION

LOWER-LEVEL FLOOR PLAN

SECTION FACING EAST

RESIDENCE AT NORTH YORK
ONTARIO, CANADA

0 4 8 16 24 feet

EARLY HOUSES

Wiseman Residence
Montauk, New York, 1965–67

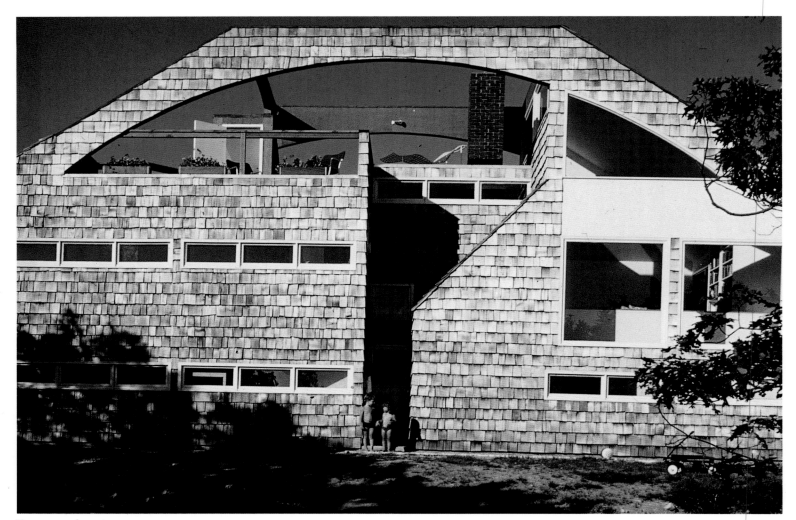

Entrance elevation

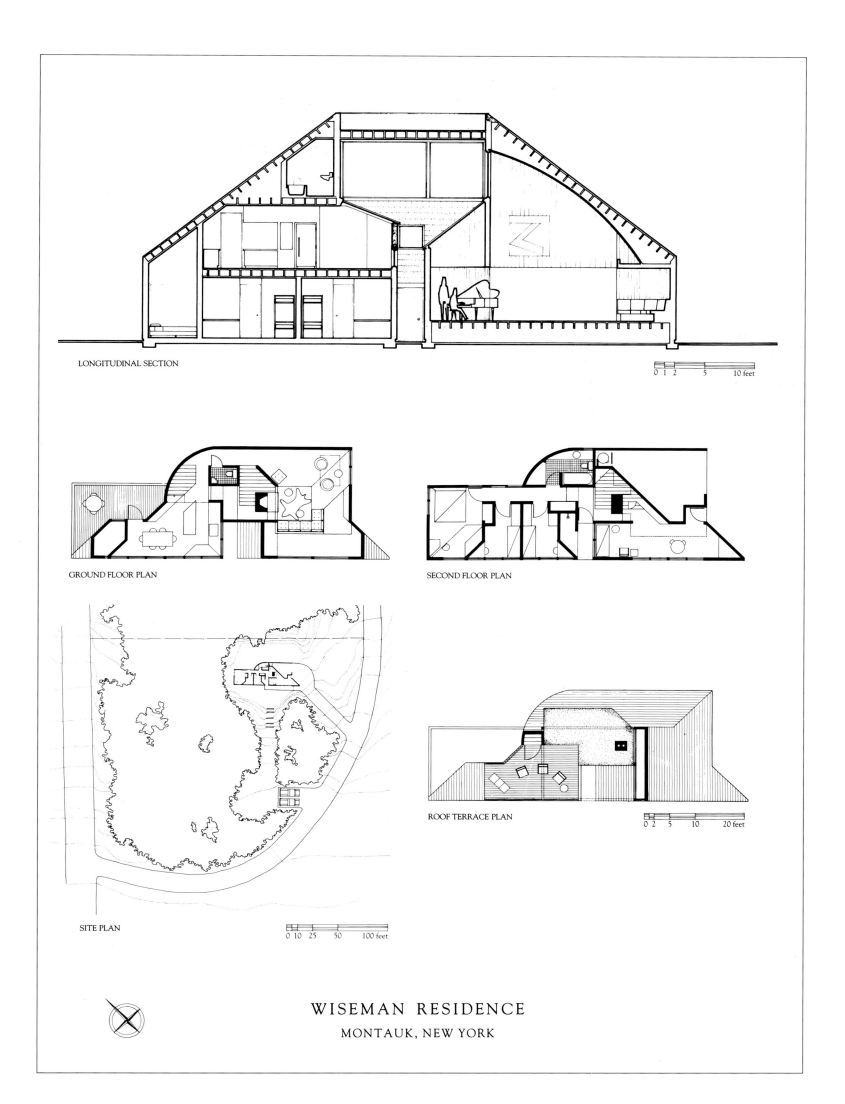

LONGITUDINAL SECTION

0 1 2   5   10 feet

GROUND FLOOR PLAN

SECOND FLOOR PLAN

SITE PLAN

0 10 25   50   100 feet

ROOF TERRACE PLAN

0 2   5   10   20 feet

WISEMAN RESIDENCE
MONTAUK, NEW YORK

View from beach

Residence
Montauk, New York, 1971–72

Pool courtyard

Guest cottage

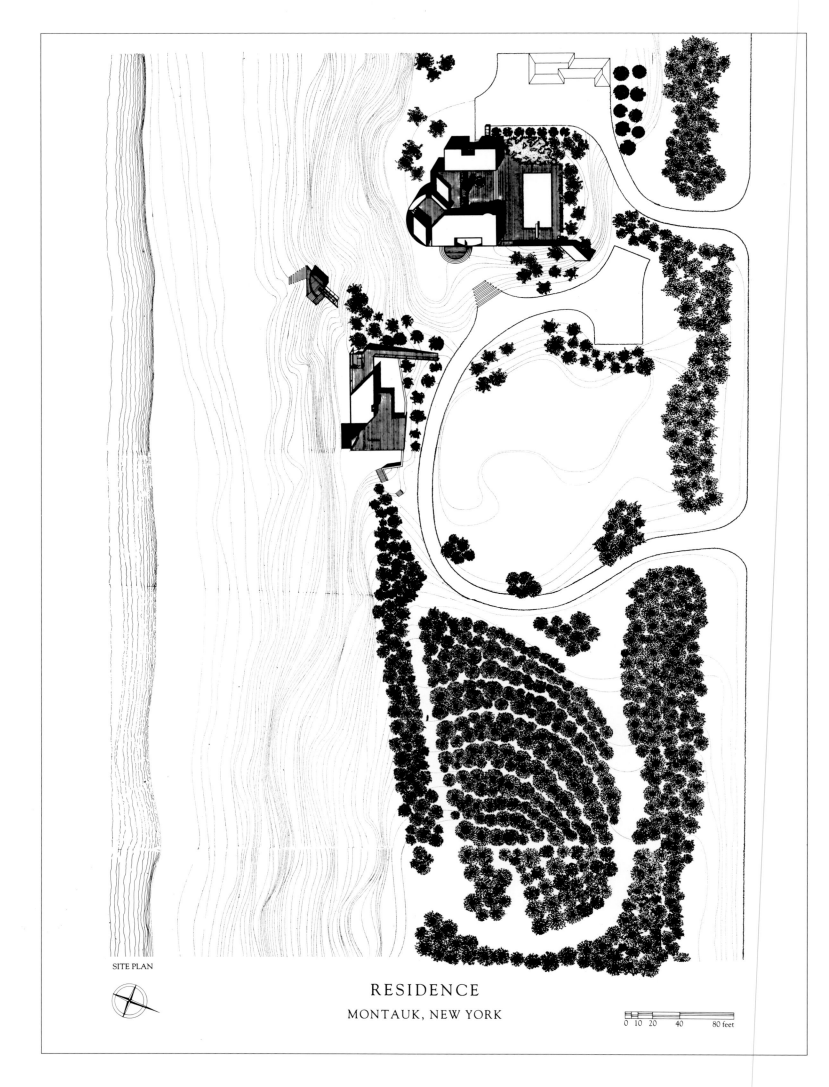

SITE PLAN

RESIDENCE

MONTAUK, NEW YORK

0 10 20   40   80 feet

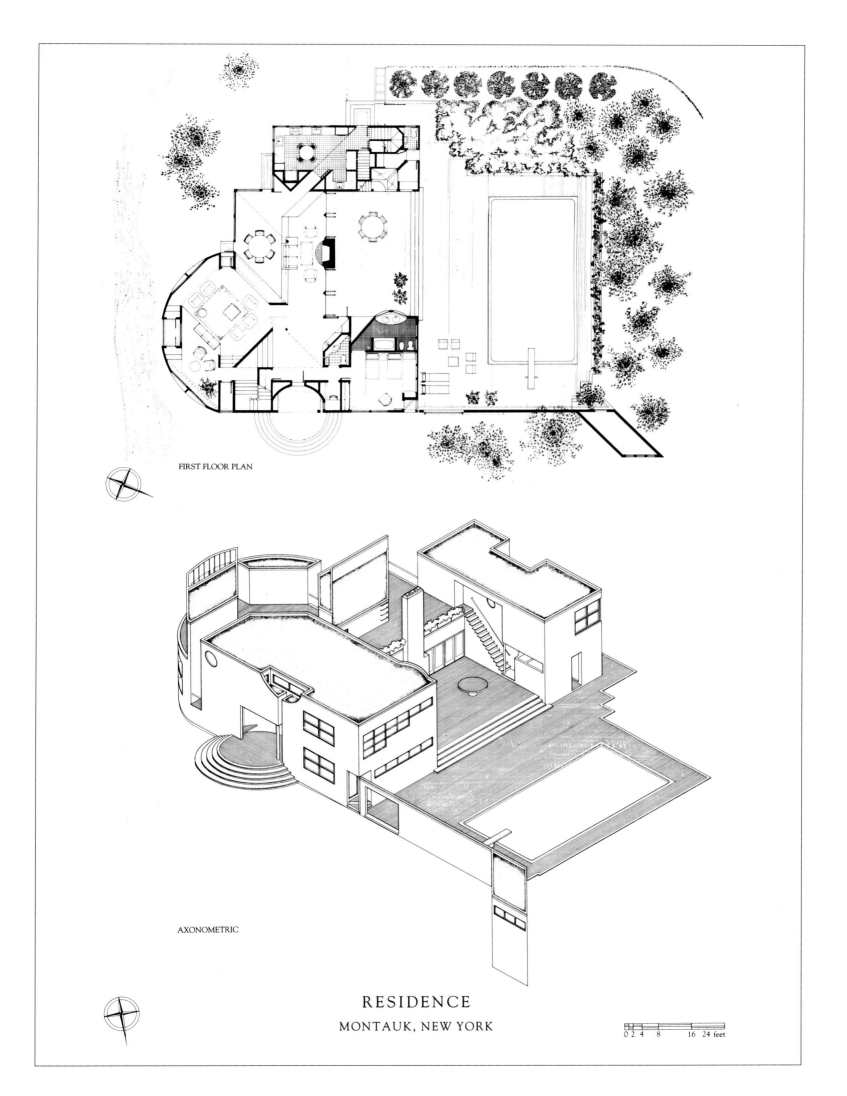

FIRST FLOOR PLAN

AXONOMETRIC

RESIDENCE

MONTAUK, NEW YORK

0 2 4   8   16 24 feet

Poolhouse
Greenwich, Connecticut, 1973–74

View from southwest

Detail of skylight

South elevation

Lang Residence
Washington, Connecticut, 1973–74

Entrance facade

East elevation

View from west

New York Townhouse
New York, New York, 1973–75

Street facade

View from living room

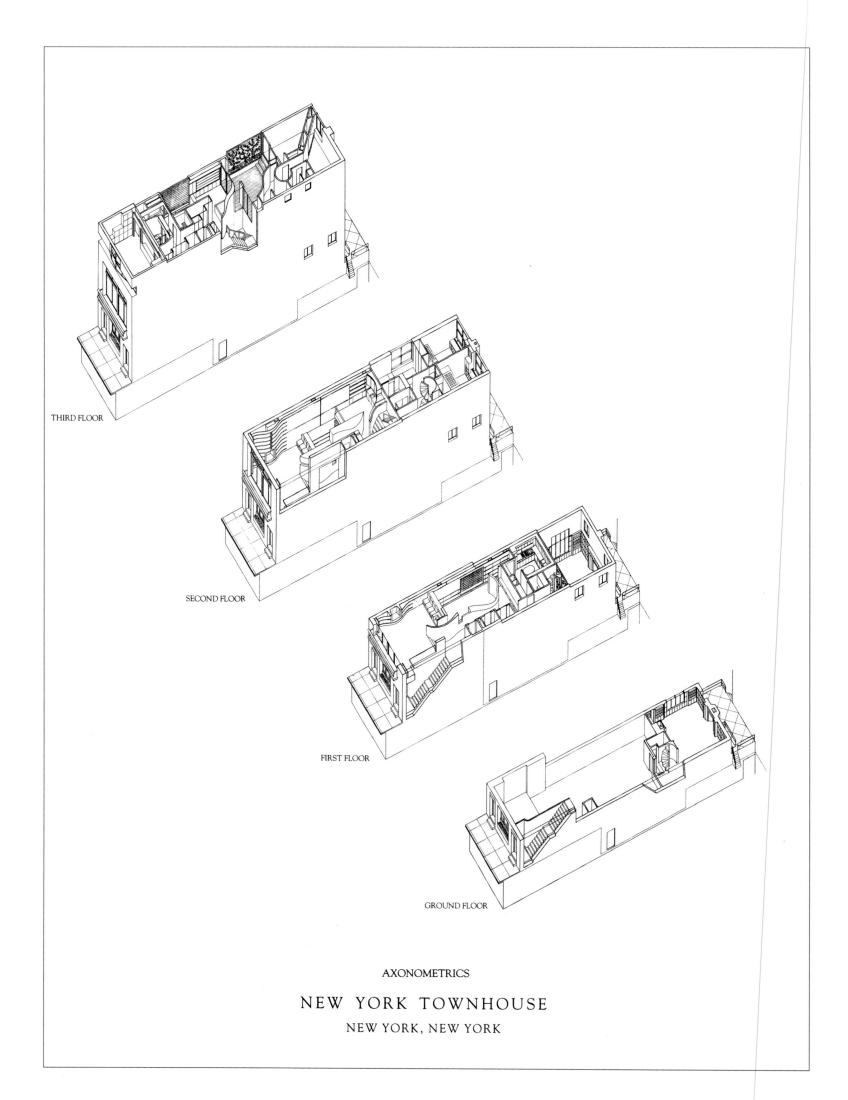

THIRD FLOOR

SECOND FLOOR

FIRST FLOOR

GROUND FLOOR

AXONOMETRICS

NEW YORK TOWNHOUSE

NEW YORK, NEW YORK

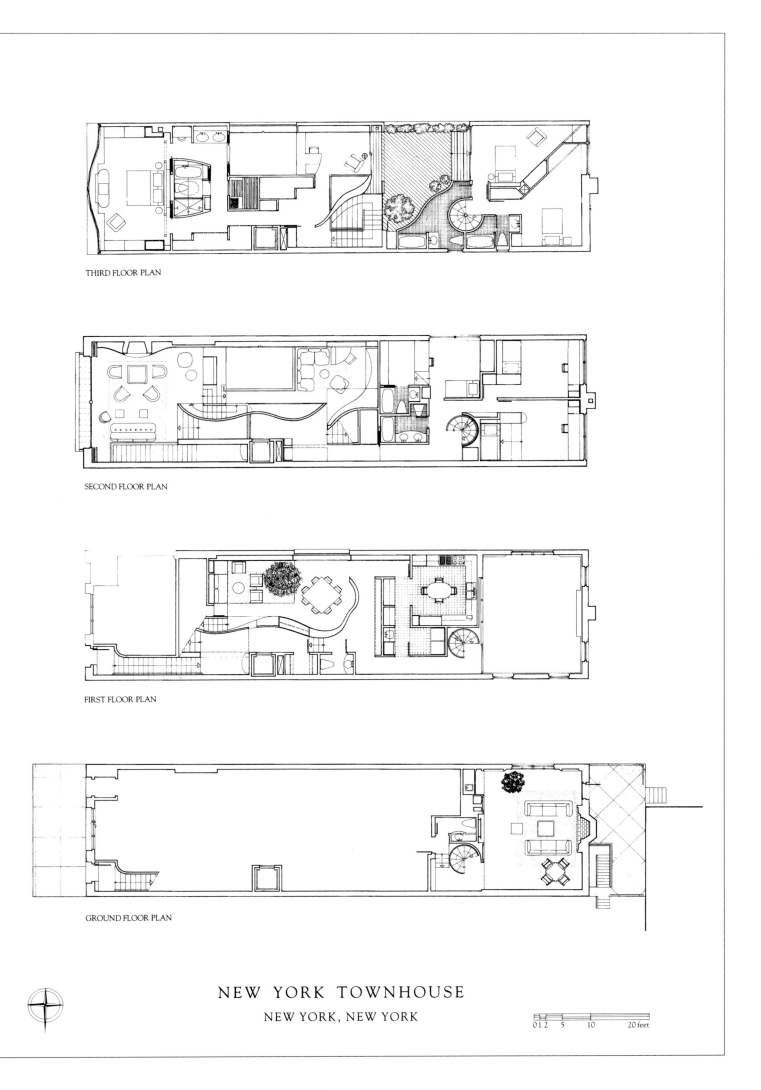

THIRD FLOOR PLAN

SECOND FLOOR PLAN

FIRST FLOOR PLAN

GROUND FLOOR PLAN

NEW YORK TOWNHOUSE
NEW YORK, NEW YORK

0 1 2   5   10   20 feet

Residence
Westchester County, New York, 1974–76

View looking northwest from pool

Detail of screen wall

South elevation

SITE PLAN

RESIDENCE

WESTCHESTER COUNTY, NEW YORK

0 20 40 80   160 240 feet

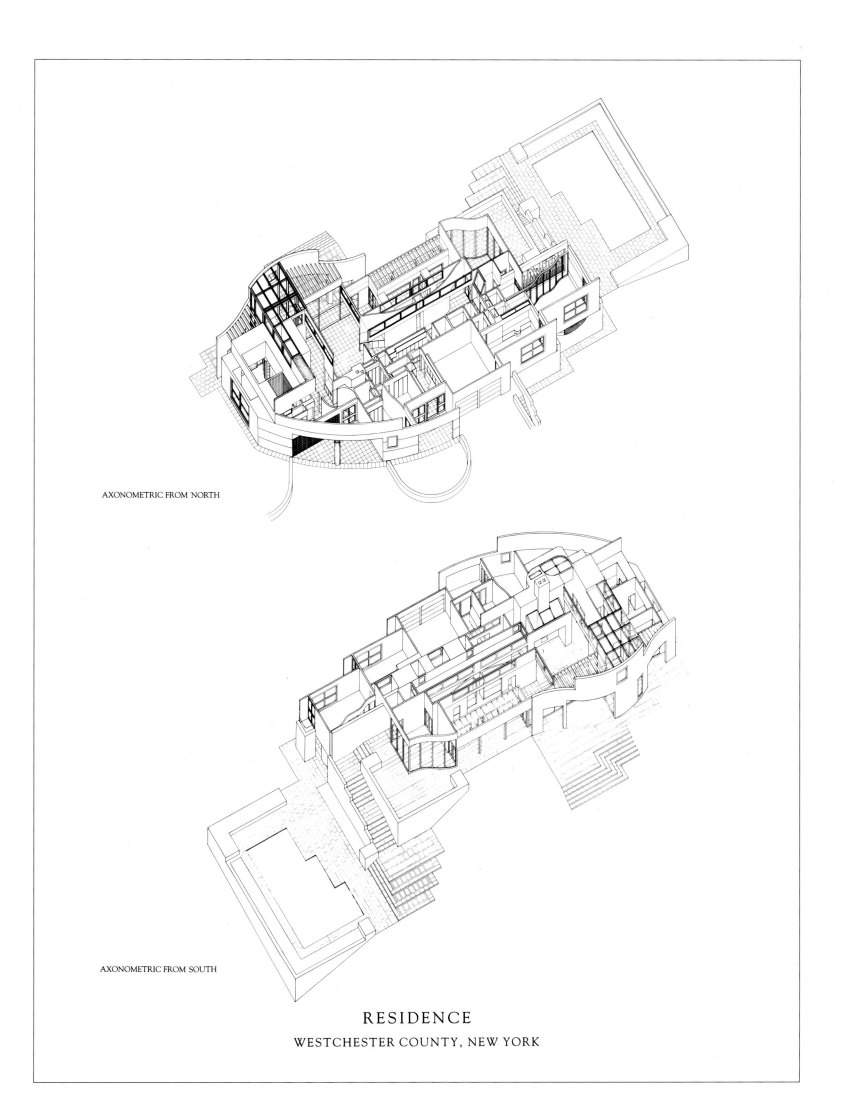

AXONOMETRIC FROM NORTH

AXONOMETRIC FROM SOUTH

RESIDENCE
WESTCHESTER COUNTY, NEW YORK

View from living room to pergola

Guest bedroom

View into winter garden

Points of View
Mount Desert Island, Maine, 1975–76

South elevation

View toward entrance

View from cove

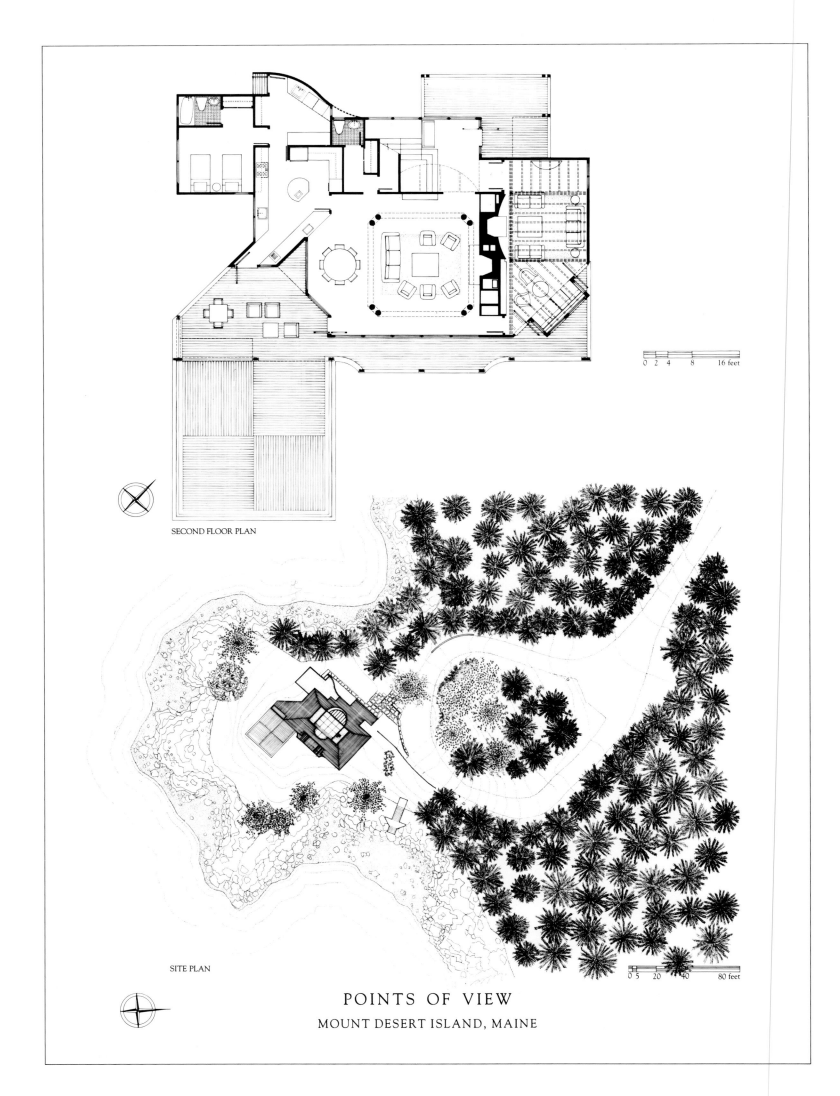

SECOND FLOOR PLAN

0 2 4 8 16 feet

SITE PLAN

0 5 20 40 80 feet

POINTS OF VIEW

MOUNT DESERT ISLAND, MAINE

Detail of porch

Carriage House
East Hampton, New York, 1975–77

Screened porch

Living room

South elevation

ANNOTATED
PROJECT LIST

Country and Suburban Houses

Residence
Llewellyn Park, New Jersey
1979–81

Architect-in-Charge: Anthony Cohn
Assistants: Ethelind Coblin, Alan Gerber,
Gavin Macrae-Gibson
Landscape Architect: Peter Rolland and
Associates
Interior Design Assistant: Alan Gerber

*This project consists of two components: the
renovation of a Georgian-style house and
the addition of a new indoor swimming pool.
The house was built in 1929, a watershed year in
the modern movement, yet it showed no awareness
of modernism. Our clients, however, were very
modern-minded. The strategy was to break open
the closed plan of the original structure with a free
plan, thereby bringing two historical styles, once
seen as mutually exclusive opposites, into a
dialogue, if not necessarily a synthesis. The
poolhouse is treated as a grotto that marks a
transition between the house and the garden.*

Robert Jensen and Patricia Conway,
*Ornamentalism: The New Decorativeness in
Architecture and Design* (New York: Clarkson
N. Potter, 1982), 24–29.

Douglas Brenner, "A Villa in Three Acts,"
Architectural Record 170 (June 1982): 120–25.

"Brighton Lively—Architect Robert Stern's
Poolhouse Fantasy," *House & Garden* 155
(January 1983): 106–15.

"Residence and Pool House, Llewellyn Park,
New Jersey, 1981–1982," *Architectural Design*
53 (July/August 1983): 66–69.

Charles Jencks, *The Language of Post-Modern
Architecture,* 4th rev. ed. (New York: Rizzoli
International Publications, 1984), 155.

"New Jersey Poolhouse," *Domus* 652 (July–
August 1984): 42–47.

Charles Jencks, *Architecture Today,* 2d rev. ed.
(London: Academy Editions, 1988), 145–46.

Awards: Distinguished Architecture Award,
New York Chapter, American Institute of
Architects, 1982; Lumen Award, New York
Section, Illuminating Engineering Society and
International Association of Lighting
Designers, 1982.

Residence
Mill Neck, New York
1981–83

Architect-in-Charge: Charles D. Warren
Assistants: Alan Gerber, John Ike
Landscape Architect: Lois Sherr
Interior Design Assistant: Alan Gerber

*Located on a bluff overlooking Oyster Bay, this
house, inspired by Edwin Lutyens's Tigbourne
Court, combines a tightly contained, triple-gabled
entrance facade with a pavilionated massing
toward the garden and the water. The plan is
organized along a generously proportioned gallery
running north-south; the major rooms open off this
gallery to the east and west. The courtyards not
only foster outdoor living but also ensure south
light in the principal rooms.*

Stanley Tigerman, "Villa with a View:
Melding Traditions on Oyster Bay,"
Architectural Digest 42 (November 1985):
132–41.

Kurt Gustmann, "Villa Mit Zwei Gesichtern,"
Häuser (February 1987): 114–21.

Awards: Honorable Mention in Design, New
York State Association of Architects,
American Institute of Architects, 1986.

Residence at Hardscrabble
East Hampton, New York
1983–85

Architect-in-Charge: Armand LeGardeur
Assistants: Kerry Moran, Kaarin Taipale
Landscape Associate: Robert Ermerins
Interior Design Associate: Ronne Fisher

*Sited just below the crest of the area's highest ridge,
this house takes advantage of the topography to
locate the principal living functions on the middle
level. The downstairs is reserved for the guest and
children's bedrooms, the upstairs for the master
suite, which is tucked under the roof. In keeping
with the rugged character of the site, the trim has*

been painted dark green and granite has been used
at the ground floor.

Carol Vogel, "Out of Sight," *New York Times
Magazine* (June 14, 1987): 58–62.

Elaine Markoutsas, "Details, Details," *Chicago
Tribune* (October 15, 1989), XV: 1, 4.

Awards: Excellence in Architecture Award,
Long Island Chapter, American Institute of
Architects, 1987; Merit Award, American
Wood Council Design Award, 1988.

Residence at Pottersville
Bedminster Township, New Jersey
1985–88

Architect-in-Charge: Randy M. Correll
Assistants: Deirdre O'Farrelly, Olivia Rowan
Landscape Architect: John Charles Smith
Interior Design Associate: Randy M. Correll

*This house nestles into the brow of a low ridge in a
landscape of rolling meadows in rural New Jersey.
Entered from the west on the short elevation, the
house opens on its south side to a sunken garden
and distant views beyond; on the east it overlooks a
meadow. On the north side, where the site's slope
permits a stone basement story, the scale is
heightened by juxtaposing the gambrel roof with
an octagonal stair tower that recalls similar
arrangements in neighboring barns and silos.*

Steven M.L. Aronson, "Architecture: Robert
A.M. Stern," *Architectural Digest* 48
(December 1991).

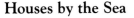

Houses by the Sea

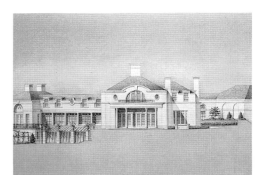

Residence
Chestnut Hill, Massachusetts
1986–91

Architects-in-Charge: Armand LeGardeur,
Charles D. Warren
Senior Assistant: Mark Johnson
Assistants: Thomas Gay, Laurie Kerr, Elizabeth
A. Kozarec, Rosamund Young
Landscape Architect: Morgan Wheelock
Interior Design Associate: Raul Morillas
Interior Design Assistants: Stephan Johnson,
Sharon Pett, Patricia Burns

*Sited at the crest of a hill, this house terminates a
long rising drive across a recently subdivided,
historically important estate. An axial sequence
leads from a circular motor court to the groin-
vaulted living room. A cross-axis connects the
library with the west garden a story below. The
wings contain the more informal living spaces as
well as extensive athletic facilities. The south and
west facades have a larger scale than the entrance
facade and provide focus and definition to the
established landscape park.*

Residence at River Oaks
Houston, Texas
1988–91

Architect-in-Charge: Roger H. Seifter
Senior Assistant: John Berson
Assistants: Abigail Huffman, Kristin
McMahon, Daniel Romauldez
Associate Architect: Richard Fitzgerald and
Associates
Landscape Associate: Robert Ermerins
Landscape Assistant: Laura Schoenbaum
Interior Design Associate: Raul Morillas
Interior Design Assistants: Paul McDonnell,
Alice Yiu

*The principal axis of this house runs roughly east-
west, overlooking the Buffalo Bayou. South light is
admitted through windows opening onto courtyards
that are walled against the entrance drive. The
gardens extend the house's geometry to incorporate
a tennis court and a swimming pool set inside a
tentlike cage of mosquito netting.*

Residence
East Quogue, New York
1979–81

Architect-in-Charge: John Averitt
Assistants: Terry Brown, John Krieble, Charles
D. Warren

*The design of this house, located on a typical
narrow seaside lot, connects with the traditions
of the Shingle Style "beach cottages" that once
proliferated along the East Coast. The overscaled
front steps lead to the principal floor at the level of
the dune. Guest bedrooms below are tucked behind
the dune, while above, the master suite under the
roof is lit by a boldly arched window that gives the
house grand scale from the beach.*

Paolo Portoghesi, *After Modern Architecture*
(New York: Rizzoli International Publications,
1980), 63.

Allan Greenberg, "Recent Houses by Robert
Stern," *Architecture and Urbanism, Extra
Edition: The Residential Works of Robert A.M.
Stern* (July 1982): 155–56.

Gavin Macrae-Gibson, "Robert Stern and the
Tradition of the Picturesque," *Architecture and
Urbanism* 179 (August 1985): 83–90.

Paul Goldberger, *The Houses of the Hamptons*
(New York: Alfred A. Knopf, 1986), cover,
30–31, 192–95.

Awards: Distinguished Architecture Award,
New York Chapter, American Institute of
Architects, 1984.

Residence at Chilmark
Martha's Vineyard, Massachusetts
1979–83

Architect-in-Charge: Roger H. Seifter
Senior Assistant: John Krieble
Interior Design Associate: Alan Gerber

*This low-slung shingled house, with its gently
flared hipped roof, dormers, bay windows, and
subsumed porches, crowns one of the highest sites
on Martha's Vineyard, commanding water views
in three directions. Inside, the effect is at once
intimate and expansive, combining bleached wood-
paneled walls, low beamed ceilings, wooden
country furniture, and comfortable upholstery.*

Paolo Portoghesi, *After Modern Architecture*
(New York: Rizzoli International Publications,
1980), 63.

Allan Greenberg, "Recent Houses by Robert
Stern," *Architecture and Urbanism, Extra
Edition: The Residential Works of Robert A.M.
Stern* (July 1982): 155–56.

"Robert A.M. Stern: Residence at Chilmark,
Martha's Vineyard," *Architectural Design* 54
(November/December 1984): 70–71.

Vincent Scully, "Architecture: Robert A.M.
Stern," *Architectural Digest* 41 (June 1984):
136–41, 164, 166.

Robert Campbell, "Shingle Style Reinvented:
Residence at Chilmark: Robert A.M. Stern,"
Architecture 74 (May 1985): 262–67; reprinted
in *Architecture Quarterly* (Fall 1985): 18–23,
and in *American Architecture of the 1980s*
(Washington, D.C.: American Institute of
Architects Press, 1990), 174–77.

Vincent Scully, *American Architecture and
Urbanism*, rev. ed. (New York: Henry Holt
& Co., 1988), 263.

Awards: Distinguished Architecture Award,
New York Chapter, American Institute of
Architects, 1984; National Honor Award,
American Institute of Architects, 1985.

Residence at Farm Neck
Martha's Vineyard, Massachusetts
1980–83

Architect-in-Charge: Roger H. Seifter
Assistant: John Krieble
Interior Design Associate: Ronne Fisher

*Responding to the large, open site facing a bay
and the ocean across a golf course, this design
gathers together the disparate components of its
particularly complex program under a large gable
form, like that of McKim, Mead and White's Low
House (1887). The clarity of the gable form lends
an imposing scale that is enhanced by the near-
symmetry of the principal facade and the
pronounced silhouette of the chimneys and
dormers.*

Allan Greenberg, "Recent Houses by Robert Stern," *Architecture and Urbanism, Extra Edition: The Residential Works of Robert A.M. Stern* (July 1982): 155–56.

Hugh Newell Jacobsen, "Architecture: Robert A.M. Stern," *Architectural Digest* 42 (May 1985): 210–19, 268.

Heinrich Klotz, *The History of Postmodern Architecture* (Cambridge, Mass.: MIT Press, 1988), 433.

Awards: Award for Excellence in Design, New York State Association of Architects, 1985; Distinguished Architecture Award, New York Chapter, American Institute of Architects, 1986.

Residence
East Hampton, New York
1980–83

Architect-in-Charge: Roger H. Seifter
Assistant: Terry Brown
Landscape Architect: Jane Lappin
Interior Design Associate: Ronne Fisher

In the heart of East Hampton's traditional summer colony, this house takes its cues from the Shingle Style "cottages" characteristic of the neighborhood, combining classical and vernacular elements. Though bold in scale, the house does not flaunt its modernity; traditional forms are subtly modified in scale, but their representational character is retained and the massing of the house adds geometric clarity to the usually picturesque stylistic type.

Vittorio Magnago Lampugnani, *Architektur Unseres in Zeichnungen: Utopie und Realität* (Stuttgart: Verlag Gerd Hatje, 1982), 150.

Robert Hefner, Clay Lancaster, and Robert A.M. Stern, *East Hampton's Heritage* (New York: W. W. Norton & Co., 1982), 206.

Douglas Brenner, "Bozzi House, East Hampton, New York," *Architectural Record* 172 (mid-April 1984): 108–11.

Paul Goldberger, "Shingle Style Again," *House & Garden* 156 (June 1984): 168–77, 211.

Gavin Macrae-Gibson, *The Secret Life of Buildings: An American Mythology* (Cambridge, Mass.: MIT Press, 1985), 98–117.

Paul Goldberger, *The Houses of the Hamptons* (New York: Alfred A. Knopf, 1986), 31, 202–3.

Charles Jencks, *Postmodernism: The New Classicism in Art and Architecture* (New York: Rizzoli International Publications, 1987), 224.

Awards: Award for Excellence in Planning and Design, *Architectural Record Houses,* 1984; Distinguished Architecture Award, New York Chapter, American Institute of Architects, 1985.

Residence
Deal, New Jersey
1982–84

Architect-in-Charge: John Ike
Assistant: Thomas A. Kligerman
Landscape Architect: Lois Sherr
Interior Design Associate: Ronne Fisher

Facing the Atlantic Ocean, this villa-like beach house takes its stylistic cue from the Italianate houses that proliferated in the neighborhood in the early 1900s. The interior planning and detailing reinforce the theme, with the combined living and dining areas occupying a large columniated and groin-vaulted room that is rather like a glazed-in loggia.

Vincent Scully, "Architecture: Robert A.M. Stern," *Architectural Digest* 43 (March 1986): 108–15.

Residence
Hewlett Harbor, New York
1984–88

Architect-in-Charge: Charles D. Warren
Assistants: Re Hagele, Armand LeGardeur, Grant Marani, Jenny Peng, Elizabeth Thompson
Landscape Associate: Robert Ermerins
Interior Design Associate: Lisa Maurer

Located between a golf course across the street in the front and a navigable channel that opens to

Hewlett Bay in the back, this house is approached by a short driveway terminating in a brick-walled courtyard. Inside, the boldly scaled classical detailing complements the generously proportioned plan and the play of natural light.

Residence
Marblehead, Massachusetts
1984–87

Architect-in-Charge: Roger H. Seifter
Senior Assistant: Caroline Hancock
Assistant: Kaarin Taipale

This house is set on a steeply sloped site with northern views toward the water. It continues in the tradition of stone-and-timber cottages that characterized development along Boston's North Shore as well as the rest of coastal New England before the turn of the century. As the land falls away, the house's rubble stone foundation emerges, a high base anchoring the more finely detailed and picturesquely massed shingled superstructure.

Sunstone
Quogue, New York
1984–87

Architect-in-Charge: Randy M. Correll
Assistants: Thomas Nohr, Constance Treadwell
Landscape Architect: Edmund Hollander
Interior Design: Parish-Hadley Associates, Inc.

A cubic mass, this house reaches out to the water with a two-story lighthouse-like tower at the southwest corner to provide the principal rooms with a panoramic view of Shinnecock Bay. The large gambrel roof sweeps down over the verandas that encircle the house and affords the interior rooms comforting shade from the summer sun.

Carol Vogel, "The Home Team," *New York Times Magazine* (August 5, 1990): 54–59.

Residence at Calf Creek
Water Mill, New York
1984–87

Architect-in-Charge: Armand LeGardeur
Senior Assistant: Luis Rueda-Salazar
Landscape Associate: Robert Ermerins
Interior Design Associate: Lisa Maurer

Located along a tributary of Mecox Bay, this house takes on a linear massing to introduce west light and water views into the principal rooms. The gambrel roof, dormer windows, and projecting bays are used in combination with more formal classical elements, including a stylobate, Tuscan columns, and a fully articulated entablature.

Kurt Andersen, "Robert A.M. Stern: New Interpretation of the Shingle Style on Long Island," *Architectural Digest* 46 (August 1989): 66–71, 94, 98.

Awards: Citation, Long Island Chapter, American Institute of Architects, 1988; Excellence in Design Award, New York State Association of Architects, American Institute of Architects, 1989.

Residence at Wilderness Point
Fishers Island, New York
1986–89

Architect-in-Charge: Randy M. Correll
Assistants: Yvonne Galindo, James Joseph
Landscape Associate: Robert Ermerins
Landscape Assistants: Stephanie Abrams, William Skelsey
Interior Design: McMillen, Inc.

This house stretches along a ridge overlooking the Long Island Sound and adjoining wetlands. In order to allow the sea breezes to circulate freely through the rooms and to admit views on every side, the house is only one room deep, making for a long central mass, to which pavilions and elements such as a tower and a gazebo have been added to form an asymmetrical and picturesque composition.

Clive Aslet, "Architecture: Robert A.M. Stern," *Architectural Digest* 48 (July 1991): 88–95.

Awards: Excellence in Design Award, New York State Association of Architects, American Institute of Architects, 1990.

Residence
Elberon, New Jersey
1985–89

Architect-in-Charge: John Ike
Project Associate: Augusta Barone
Assistants: Charles Barrett, Grant Marani, Pat Tiné
Landscape Associate: Robert Ermerins
Landscape Assistant: Stephanie Abrams
Interior Design Associate: Lisa Maurer
Interior Design Assistant: Alice Yiu

This seaside villa is composed of simple stucco volumes enriched by stone and terra-cotta details and capped by red tile roofs. Entered through a cloistered courtyard that provides afternoon light to the dining room while screening it from the parking area, the house opens toward the beach across broad limestone terraces and a tiered swimming pool that appears to flow into the ocean.

Mildred F. Schmertz, "Palm Beach North," *House & Garden* 163 (July 1991): 112–19, 126.

Villa in New Jersey
1983–89

Architect-in-Charge: Thomas A. Kligerman
Assistants: Augusta Barone, Victoria Casasco, Arthur Chabon, Berndt Dams, William T. Georgis, Natalie Jacobs, Laurie Kerr, Françoise Sogno
Landscape Associate: Robert Ermerins
Interior Design Assistants: Ingrid Armstrong, Stephan Johnson, Tanya Kelly, Lisa Maurer

Located among turn-of-the-century Italianate villas of a former resort colony, this house explores the integration of classical architecture and landscape. The house is not a singular object set against nature but a group of pavilions overlooking a series of gardens. The principal mass, containing rooms for formal entertaining and the bedrooms, opens onto a sunken garden to the south, where telescoping walls and stepped grass terraces rising toward a granite basin visually lengthen the view.

Giancarlo Priori, "Ritrovare I Propri Dei," *Eupalino* 9/10 (1987–88): 31–36.

Robert Campbell, "Remaking the Mediterranean Style," *Architectural Digest* 47 (December 1990): 102–11.

Awards: Award for Unbuilt Projects, New York Chapter, American Institute of Architects, 1985.

Houses in the Mountains

Sky View
Aspen, Colorado
1987–90

Architect-in-Charge: Armand LeGardeur
Assistants: Karen Small, Derrick Smith
Landscape Associate: Robert Ermerins
Landscape Assistant: William Skelsey
Interior Design: Jessup, Inc.

This house, located at the topmost reaches of Red Mountain, commands a spectacular view of Aspen and its ski slopes. It is organized as a series of volumes clad in sandstone, stucco, and wood, with the principal rooms opening off a dramatic stair that leads down the slope from the formal entrance at the top.

Spruce Lodge
Old Snowmass, Colorado
1987–91

Architect-in-Charge, Design and Construction Documents: Thomas A. Kligerman
Architect-in-Charge, Construction: Arthur Chabon
Assistants: Silvina Goefron, Abigail Huffman, Valerie Hughes, Timothy Haines, Robert Miller, Warren Van Wees
Landscape Associate: Robert Ermerins
Landscape Assistant: William Skelsey
Interior Design Associate: Raul Morillas
Interior Design Assistants: Deborah Emery, Stephan Johnson, Nancy Boszhardt

From a knoll in a valley this house offers a magnificent view of mountains and river. Picturesquely massed, it synthesizes two forms of rustic architecture: that of the Adirondack camp and that of the Rocky Mountain ranch. As in its predecessors, the heavy-timber trussed living room, with its Colorado sandstone fireplace, French doors, and double-height windows that frame the view, serves as a grand gathering space at the heart of the house.

Houses in Town

Residence
Brooklyn, New York
1983–86

Architect-in-Charge: Alan Gerber
Assistants: Anthony Cohn, David Eastman, William Georgis, Warren A. James, Kristin McMahon
Landscape Associate: Robert Ermerins
Interior Design Associate: Alan Gerber

Built on a narrow lot in an established neighborhood, this house creates its unique identity by refining, not rejecting, the architectural themes and materials that typify its neighbors. The constricted space is perceptually enlarged by the enfilade of principal rooms, leading from the front of the lot to the garden at the back, and by the two-story entrance hall at the center of the plan.

Ghisi Grütter, *Il Disegno degli Architetti Americani Contemporanei* (Rome: Gangemi Editore, 1987), 134–38.

Heinrich Klotz, ed., *New York Architektur, 1970–1990* (Munich: Deutsches Architekturmuseum Prestel-Verlag, 1989), 220–21.

Awards: Award for Unbuilt Projects, New York Chapter, American Institute of Architects, 1985.

Residence on Russian Hill
San Francisco, California
1985–89

Architect-in-Charge: Alan Gerber
Project Associates: Kristin McMahon, Elizabeth Thompson
Assistant: Ken McIntyre-Horito
Associated Architect: Richard Hannum
Landscape Architect: Mai K. Arbegast
Interior Design: Randolph Arczynski

This extensive reconstruction and expansion of one of the oldest houses on Russian Hill consists of two significant compositional strategies: the

construction of a belvedere-like entrance tower at the northwest corner; and the insertion of a toplit staircase into the center of the house, which leads visitors to the principal living rooms on the top floor and the spectacular views of San Francisco they offer.

Paul Goldberger, "Architecture: Robert A.M. Stern," *Architectural Digest* 47 (October 1990): 196–205.

Sally Woodbridge, "Rising to the Occasion," *Progressive Architecture* 71 (November 1990): 80–85.

Residence at North York
Ontario, Canada
1988–

Architect-in-Charge: Roger H. Seifter
Project Associate: Kristin McMahon
Senior Assistant: Diane Smith
Assistants: Abigail Huffman, Olivia Rowan
Associated Architect: Gabor & Popper
Landscape Associate: Robert Ermerins
Landscape Assistants: Charlotte Frieze, Laura Schoenbaum

Located on a double lot in one of Toronto's oldest suburbs, this house employs a French Norman vocabulary of rubble stone walls, wood casement windows, and steeply pitched slate roofs. Its composition of semidiscrete pavilions arranged formally about a central mass reduces the apparent bulk of the house and contributes to the picturesque aspect of the exterior.

Early Houses

Wiseman Residence
Montauk, New York
1965–67

A work of brash youth—it was Stern's first house—this residence confronts a taut shoreline from a high wooded site. The boldly scaled gabled mass was influenced by the work of Robert Venturi and the desire to break with the dematerialized abstraction of the then-prevalent late International Style.

Alice D. Runge, "Cutout Facade," *Progressive Architecture* 50 (June 1969): 110–15.

Elizabeth Sverbeyeff, "Arcs & Bridges—The Breakaway Feeling," *House Beautiful* 111 (August 1969): 70–73.

Vincent Scully, *The Shingle Style Today or the Historian's Revenge* (New York: George Braziller, 1974), 32, 107–8.

Paul Goldberger, *The Houses of the Hamptons* (New York: Alfred A. Knopf, 1986), 26–27, 198.

Paul Goldberger, "Variations on a Theme," *New York Times Magazine* (October 16, 1988): 32–36.

Residence
Montauk, New York
1971–72

Assistants: John Anhorn, Daniel L. Colbert

An integrated complex of three buildings winding down a fifty-foot cliff, this project marks the architect's first attempt to deal with a group of buildings.

Gerald Allen, "Mapping Out Realms for the Body and Mind and Memory," *Architectural Record* 154 (September 1973): 133–40.

Vincent Scully, *The Shingle Style Today or the Historian's Revenge* (New York: George Braziller, 1974), 33, 109.

Paul Goldberger, *The Houses of the Hamptons* (New York: Alfred A. Knopf, 1986), 204–7.

Awards: Excellence in Residential Design, New York Chapter, American Institute of Architects, 1973.

Poolhouse
Greenwich, Connecticut
1973–74

Assistant-in-Charge: Daniel L. Colbert
Assistants: Joan Chan, Ronne Fisher, William Schweber, Clifford M. Thacher-Renshaw
Landscape Architect: Peter Rolland and Associates

Though physically attached to the main house by means of walls and an enclosed service passageway, this pavilion and bathhouse seem completely separate. A sculptural solution is achieved by working with the same family of forms that govern the design of the main house but shaping them in an exaggerated way.

Robert A.M. Stern, "A Serious Discussion of an Apparently Whimsical House," *Architectural Record* 158 (July 1975): 99–104.

"Add On for Escape: A Getaway Poolhouse," *House & Garden* 148 (June 1976): 100–105.

Charles Jencks, *The Language of Post-Modern Architecture*, rev. ed. (New York: Rizzoli International Publications, 1977), 122–23.

Paolo Portoghesi, *After Modern Architecture* (New York: Rizzoli International Publications, 1980), xiv, 64.

Charles Jencks, *Architecture Today*, 2d rev. ed. (London: Academy Editions, 1988), 122, 125.

Lang Residence
Washington, Connecticut
1973–74

Assistant-in-Charge: Jeremy P. Lang
Assistant: Edmund H. Stoecklein
Landscape Architect: Daniel Stewart

A small house made to seem quite grand, this residence was a landmark in its own way. It marked the architect's first exploration of classical detail and historical reference, each tackled in a deliberately self-conscious way.

Charles W. Moore, "Lang Residence: Where Are We Now, Vincent Scully?" *Progressive Architecture* 56 (April 1975); cover, 78–83.

Charles Jencks, *The Language of Post-Modern Architecture* (New York: Rizzoli International Publications, 1977), 88.

Charles Jencks, "More Modern than Modern," *The Sunday Times Magazine*, London (May 29, 1977): 30–31.

Paolo Portoghesi, *After Modern Architecture* (New York: Rizzoli International Publications, 1980), xiii–xiv, 64.

Paolo Portoghesi, *Postmodern: The Architecture of the Post-Industrial Society* (New York: Rizzoli International Publications, 1983), 39.

Charles Jencks, *Architecture Today*, 2d rev. ed. (London: Academy Editions, 1988), 200–202.

Heinrich Klotz, *The History of Postmodern Architecture* (Cambridge, Mass.: MIT Press, 1988), 191–92.

Awards: Excellence in Residential Design, New York Chapter, American Institute of Architects, 1975; Award of Merit, American Institute of Architects in cooperation with *House and Home*, 1977.

New York Townhouse
New York, New York
1973–75

Assistant-in-Charge: Jeremy P. Lang
Assistants: Wayne Berg, Ronne Fisher,
Laurence Marner

This townhouse, located on one of New York City's most prominent avenues, was completely reconstructed. Though the use of classical detail in the facade is tentative, there is enough detail and compositional order to permit an aesthetic conversation with the traditional apartment houses that form the context.

Sharon Lee Ryder, "Stern Dimensions," *Progressive Architecture* 57 (June 1976): 70–77.

Paul Goldberger, "Robert A.M. Stern's Two Houses," *Architecture and Urbanism* 82 (September 1977): 73–92.

"World: Stern Hybrids," *Architectural Review* 162 (December 1977): 331–33.

Brent Brolin, *Architecture in Context* (New York: Van Nostrand Reinhold, 1980), 128–29.

David Dunster, *Key Buildings of the 20th Century, 2: Houses 1945–1989* (New York: Rizzoli International Publications, 1990), 88–89.

Awards: Award for Excellence in Design, New York State Association of Architects, 1976; Lumen Award, New York Section, Illuminating Engineering Society and International Association of Lighting Designers, 1978; National Honor Award, American Institute of Architects, 1980.

Residence
Westchester County, New York
1974–76

Assistants-in-Charge: Daniel L. Colbert, Jeremy P. Lang
Assistants: Robert Buford, Joan Chan, Ronne Fisher
Landscape Architect: Peter Rolland and Associates
Interior Design Associate: Ronne Fisher

Set on a large estate property, this sprawling one-story villa attempts to synthesize the earthiness of Tuscany with the casual space-making of 1930s California modernism.

"Letting Go with Color: Architecture," *House & Garden* 148 (September 1976): 70–71, 82–85.

Frank E. Sanchis, *American Architecture: Westchester County, New York—Colonial to Contemporary* (Croton-on-Hudson, N.Y.: North River Press, 1977), 168–69.

Charles Jencks, *The Language of Post-Modern Architecture,* rev. ed. (New York: Rizzoli International Publications, 1977), 118–19, 123.

Suzanne Stephens, "Grand Allusions," *Progressive Architecture* 58 (February 1977): 58–63.

Paul Goldberger, "Robert A.M. Stern's Two Houses," *Architecture and Urbanism* 82 (September 1977): 73–92.

Paolo Portoghesi, *After Modern Architecture* (New York: Rizzoli International Publications, 1980), xiii, 65.

David Mackay, *La Casa Unifamiliar/The Modern House* (Barcelona: Editorial Gustavo Gili, 1984), 150–53.

Vittorio Magnago Lampugnani, ed., *Encyclopedia of 20th Century Architecture* (New York: Harry N. Abrams, 1986), 317.

Manfredo Tafuri, *The Sphere and the Labyrinth* (Cambridge, Mass.: MIT Press, 1987), 359–60.

Charles Jencks, *Architecture Today,* 2d rev. ed. (London: Academy Editions, 1988), 200–201.

Heinrich Klotz, *The History of Postmodern Architecture* (Cambridge, Mass.: MIT Press, 1988), 191–92.

Peter Gössel and Gabriele Leuthäuser, *Architektur des 20. Jahrhunderts* (Berlin: Benedikt Taschen Verlag, 1990), 274.

Awards: Progressive Architecture, Citation, 1976; Residential Design Awards Program, New York Chapter, American Institute of Architects, 1977; First Honor Award, Homes for Better Living Awards Program, *Housing,* 1978.

Points of View
Mount Desert Island, Maine
1975–76

Assistant-in-Charge: Daniel L. Colbert

With this house the architect, inspired by the traditions of the place, made his first serious attempt to capture in a new house the qualities and details he had admired in the Shingle Style cottages of the past.

Charles K. Gandee, "Robert A.M. Stern/ Points of View, Mount Desert Island, Maine," *Architectural Record* 169 (mid-May 1981): 102–7.

Carriage House
East Hampton, New York
1975–77

Assistants: Clifford M. Thacher-Renshaw, Ronne Fisher

Though technically an alteration, this project might more accurately be described as a re-creation of a 1906 carriage house that had been virtually lost in a fire. A new screened porch, a pool, and pavilions reflect and expand upon the vocabulary of the older structure.

Dean Barry, "Architectural Ornamentation," *Residential Interiors* 4 (September/October 1979): 88–93.

Paul Goldberger, *The Houses of the Hamptons* (New York: Alfred A. Knopf, 1986), 30, 196–97.

Illustration Credits

Peter Aaron: ©ESTO: 27, 30–31, 33, 70–71, 74–75, 232; Courtesy of *Architectural Digest.* ©1985. All rights reserved: 34–35, 37–41, 84–85, 87–91; Courtesy of *Architectural Digest.* ©1984. All rights reserved: 76–77, 80–83.

Steven Brooke: 110, 114–16, 117 bottom right and left, 118–19; Courtesy of *Architectural Digest.* ©1991. All rights reserved: 48–49, 52–55, 150, 152–53, 155–57; Courtesy of *Architectural Digest.* ©1989. All rights reserved: 136–37, 140 top, 141–45; Courtesy of *Architectural Digest.* ©1990. All rights reserved: 175 top, 178 bottom, 182 top, 183–88.

William Choi: 117 top, 140 bottom.

Langdon Clay: Courtesy of *House & Garden.* ©1984 by The Condé Nast Publications Inc.: 93 bottom, 97–101.

Daniel L. Colbert: 229.

Whitney Cox: All rights reserved. 1987: 120–21, 124–25.

Mark Darley: ©ESTO: 215.

William T. Georgis: 170–71, 202.

John Hall: 42–43, 45–47.

Lizzie Himmel: 131–35.

Timothy Hursley: 174, 175 bottom, 178 top, 179, 182 bottom, 189; Courtesy of *House & Garden.* ©1991 by The Condé Nast Publications Inc.: 162–63, 166–69.

Jane Lidz: Courtesy of *Architectural Digest.* ©1990. All rights reserved: 208–9, 212–13.

Norman McGrath: ©1982: 73; Courtesy of *House & Garden.* ©1983 by The Condé Nast Publications Inc.: 32.

Hans Namuth: 222.

James V. Righter: 242 top.

Maris Semel: 224–25.

Roberto Schezen: 93 top, 96.

Tony Soluri: Courtesy of *Architectural Digest.* © 1986. All rights reserved: 102–3, 105–9.

Robert A.M. Stern Architects: 130, 151, 203, 206–7, 236 bottom.

Edmund H. Stoecklein: 26, 228 bottom, 230–31, 233, 236 top, 237, 240–41, 247.

Tim Street-Porter: ©ESTO: 246 bottom.

Y. Takase: Y. Futagawa Associates Photographers. ©Retoria: 242 bottom, 243, 245.

Tom Yee: Courtesy of *House & Garden.* ©1976 by The Condé Nast Publications Inc.: 228 top.

Andrew Zega: 56–57, 62–63, 92, 111, 126–27, 146–47, 158–59, 192–93, 196–97, 216–17.

The following people assisted in drawing the plates illustrated in this book:

Tracy Aranoff
Andres Francisco Blanco
Eileen Emmet
Silvina Goefron
Ellen Honigstock
Adonica Inzer
Ken Van Kesteren
Joel Rosenberg
Luis Rueda
John Saunders
Piroshka Savany
Oscar Shamamian
Hailim Suh
Paul Williger
Brian Yeley

Chronology of Firm
Robert A.M. Stern, 1966–69
Robert A.M. Stern and John S. Hagmann, Architects, 1969–77
Robert A.M. Stern Architects, 1977–present